ROBERT
CHAPMAN

Robert Cleaver Chapman

ROBERT
CHAPMAN

A Biography By

Robert L. Peterson

LOIZEAUX
Neptune, New Jersey

Robert Chapman
© 1995 Robert L. Peterson

A Publication of Loizeaux Brothers, Inc.,
*A Nonprofit Organization Devoted to the Lord's Work
and to the Spread of His Truth*

Unless otherwise stated,
Scripture quotations in this book
are from the King James version of the Bible.
Verses marked NASB are taken from the
New American Standard Bible.

Library of Congress Cataloging-in-Publication Data

Peterson, Robert L., 1930–
Robert Chapman / Robert L. Peterson.
Includes bibliographical references.
ISBN 0-87213-691-4 (hc: alk. paper)
1. Chapman, Robert Cleaver, 1803-1902. 2. Plymouth Brethren–
–England—Clergy—Biography.   I. Title.
BX8809.C48P48   1995
280'.4'092—dc20
[B] 95-33954

Printed in the United States of America
10 9 8 7 6 5 4 3 2 1

Contents

Preface

The remarkable Robert C. Chapman served God in an isolated corner of nineteenth-century England. He deliberately avoided publicity because he did not want to be the focus of attention that properly belonged to his Lord. Yet by the end of his life he was known throughout the world for his great love, wisdom, and compassion.

Leaders of his time commonly kept daily journals with an eye toward eventual publication. But Chapman kept no journal and destroyed practically all the correspondence he received. He permitted only one photographic portrait to be taken of himself, and that was when he was in his nineties. Only a few snapshots in which he appears exist. Even the writer of his obituary in a local newspaper noted how difficult it would be to put together a comprehensive story about his life, and this has proven to be true. A few memorials were published soon after his death in 1902, but only one short biography was written.

These facts make it difficult for the biographer to uncover the human side of this man, who was a leader yet a servant to those he led. The biographer must resist the temptation to glorify his subject and leave Chapman's faults untouched. But the faults in Chapman's life are so few and minor that an honest biography sounds almost too good. According to the statements of a multitude, Chapman was a strikingly saintly, loving, and humble man. He is an excellent role model for all who wish to follow Christ. A better example of a balanced and compassionate worker in God's church would be hard to find.

ROBERT CHAPMAN

As we follow the life of this man through his trials and triumphs, we will look at many people around him, his mentor, his companions, his adversaries, the Brethren movement, and the culture in which he lived.

Acknowledgments

I have chosen not to use footnotes in the text. However a section at the end of the book identifies my written sources and adds a few notes. About half of the material contained in this biography is derived from the principal memorial and the earlier biography (references 1 and 7). I have also obtained new material from people whose parents, grandparents, or relatives knew Chapman. Ruth Morrish, Joy Shapland, Monica Shapland, Charles Fraser-Smith, and Douglas Turner, all of Barnstaple, are among these. Mr. and Mrs. William Moase of Barnstaple supplied many details of the early days of Ebenezer Chapel.

The John Rylands University Library of Manchester in Manchester, England, contains much material on the early Christian Brethren with whom Chapman associated, and from its archives I have obtained much information through the kind assistance of Dr. David Brady. Dr. Harold Rowdon and F. Roy Coad, authors of early Brethren histories, have also been helpful to me, and I have used material from their books. Frank Holmes kindly supplied me with material that he was not able to put into a second edition of his biography, *Brother Indeed.* John Gaskin and Harold Brown of the Whitby Literary & Philosophical Society at the Whitby Museum Library in Whitby, England, have kindly supplied me with the Chapman pedigree and many other details of the Chapman family. Rev. B. A. Hopkinson, rector of the parish of Whitby, gave me valuable assistance in establishing contacts in the Whitby area. Mr. E. Dell Sewell and Stella Sewell of the Whitby Religious Society of Friends did much work in supplying information about the Quaker background of some of the Chapmans. Mr. M. J. Wickes of Bideford, England, brought my attention to the 1851 ecclesiastical census of Devon. Dr. David MacLeod of Emmaus Bible College, Dubuque, Iowa, kindly supplied interesting items.

Alex Strauch, especially, has encouraged me to write this book. His book on *Biblical Eldership* (Lewis & Roth, Denver, 1987) provides a new and detailed Scriptural basis for leadership in the local church, and I would like to think that this present volume provides a readable example of a godly leader.

To these and to all others whom I have encountered in gathering materials for this book, I give sincere thanks.

My wife Jane has been my fellow laborer in researching material for this book. She constantly encouraged me during the period of its writing. My special thanks and love are extended to her.

ROBERT L. PETERSON
BOULDER, COLORADO, 1995

Chronology

1730s	George Whitefield and John Wesley begin open-air preaching.
1780	Sunday school movement begins.
1783	Elizabeth Paget is born.
1785	James Harington Evans is born.
1789	French revolution begins.
1793	Britain and France begin war.
	Missionary William Carey sails for India.
1795	Anthony Norris Groves is born.
1796	William Hake is born.
1800	John Nelson Darby is born.
1803	Robert C. Chapman is born.
1804	British and Foreign Bible Society is formed.
1805	George Müller is born.
	Henry Craik is born.
1818	John Street Chapel is built.
1823	Robert C. Chapman is converted.
1825-1830	Brethren movement begins in southwest England and Ireland.
1832	Robert C. Chapman moves to Barnstaple and begins work at Ebenezer Chapel.
	George Müller and Henry Craik begin work in Bristol.
	J. Hudson Taylor is born.
1834	Robert C. Chapman makes first trip to Spain.
	Charles Spurgeon is born.
1838	Robert C. Chapman makes second trip to Spain.

1838	Ebenezer Chapel is relinquished to Particular Baptists.
1842	Bear Street Chapel is built.
1845	Troubles arise at Plymouth Assembly; John Nelson Darby forms new Assembly.
1848	Robert C. Chapman walks through Ireland.
1849	Brethren movement divides into two sections.
1850	James Harington Evans dies.
1853	Anthony Norris Groves dies.
1854	J. Hudson Taylor first arrives in China.
1856	Bear Street Chapel starts day school.
1863	Elizabeth Paget dies.
	Hakes move to Barnstaple.
	Robert C. Chapman makes third trip to Spain.
1865	J. Hudson Taylor founds China Inland Mission.
1866	Henry Craik dies.
1871	Robert C. Chapman makes fourth and last trip to Spain.
1882	John Nelson Darby dies.
1890	William Hake dies.
1892	Charles Spurgeon dies.
1898	George Müller dies.
1902	Robert C. Chapman dies.

1
A Glimpse at a Long Life

The old man held the arm of his walking companion as they made their way through the streets of Barnstaple on their daily walk. His short steps held little hint of the rapid gait and long strides of his earlier years when he had traversed the countryside of southwest England. "Mornin', Mr. Chapman," was a common greeting from the townspeople who met him. Robert Cleaver Chapman followed their greeting with a warm acknowledgment and often a portion of Scripture.

For seventy years he pastored in the hamlets and villages surrounding Barnstaple. With patience and gentleness he was a servant to those he led. "My business is to love others and not to seek that others shall love me" were words remembered by one of the many missionaries he had influenced.

The word *love*, which so clings to any account of Chapman's life, refers to an attitude of caring, a giving of himself that marked his long life. He understood the concept of Christian love as few others have. His life illustrated Christ's new commandment that we "love one another, even as I have loved you" (John 13:34, NASB); it was the very heartbeat of true Christianity.

Robert Chapman became one of the most respected Christians of nineteenth-century Britain. He was a lifelong friend and mentor to George Müller, the founder of the large orphanage system at Bristol. He was an adviser to J. Hudson Taylor, who used him as a referee for China Inland Mission. His acquaintance C. H. Spurgeon called him "the saintliest man I ever knew." An Anglican clergyman wrote after a stay at Chapman's rest home, "For the first time I heard Robert Chapman expound the Scriptures. Deep called to deep as he warmed to his subject. The impression made on my mind is almost all that I can remember, as I took no notes; but as his Bible closed I felt like an infant in the knowledge of God, compared with a giant like this."

A brilliant man from a wealthy family, Chapman could have chosen any number of prestigious paths to follow. Yet he chose a life of poverty. He wanted to work and live with poor and uneducated people. By seeing Christ's love in a person who loved them, they could more readily believe the gospel message.

As we trace Chapman's life, we see first a precocious child, then a teenager searching for and yet judging God. In his teens he was sent to London to become a lawyer, and there he met his Lord. After his conversion he was discipled by a preacher who had broken from the Church of England. Chapman developed a strong concern for the welfare of the dwellers in the slums of London—the same slums of which Charles Dickens wrote a few years later. Invited to pastor a troubled church in a small town, he abandoned a modest fortune, his profession, and all possibilities of advancement to spend the rest of his life in an obscure corner of England.

We see him struggle with a small group of immature Christians, bringing them to maturity through love and example. He found himself in the midst of a growing religious movement made up of many men and women with convictions similar to his own. Later he watched with grief as a portion of this movement turned inward and moved away from its initial love and openness. He was not strong enough to stop the wrenching apart, but as one of the few who were respected by many on both sides of the split, he was called upon to heal hurting souls and repair damaged congregations.

He became a missionary to missionaries. His home became a retreat for tired and discouraged Christian workers. He counseled and encouraged, always on the basis of the Scriptures he loved.

Robert Chapman was not a noted orator, but he became a good preacher; he was not known as a theologian, but he was a thorough student of the Bible; he was not famous as a hymn writer, but many of his hymns are still sung. What then made Chapman so beloved and effective in his time? Quite simply, his utter devotion to Christ and his determination to *live* Christ. These were the driving forces in his life. From these flowed his other attributes, his balanced outlook, and most of all the love for which he was best known. In return, people loved him and God honored him with good health, a long life, and inward peace.

One of the few photos taken of R.C. Chapman.

The Chapman family roots can be found in the area around Whitby, England.

The home of Robert Chapman's heart was Barnstaple.

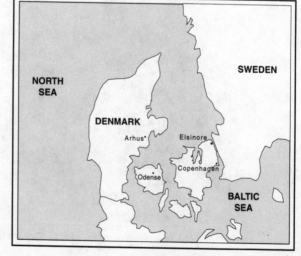

Although of English descent, Robert C. Chapman was born in Elsinore, Denmark.

2
Robert Grows Up

Those who knew Robert Chapman only as an adult were always surprised to learn that he had been born into a wealthy family. The Chapmans had been one of the dominant families in the area around Whitby, North Yorkshire, for many generations. They had taken their livelihood from the sea and the sea had brought them wealth and power. Though some had left for other pursuits, none had followed the path that Robert Cleaver Chapman would take.

Born on January 4, 1803, Robert was the sixth of ten children. At the time of his birth his parents, Thomas and Ann, lived in Elsinore (now Helsingor), Denmark, where his father ran a prosperous merchandising business (probably that of importing and exporting goods). The family lived in a large, exquisitely furnished home. A staff of servants catered to their needs, and a stable of horses and a coach bearing the family coat of arms were reminders of life back in Yorkshire—the center of the Chapman family interests. (See appendix A for more details of the Chapman family history.)

Ann, the mother of all these children, seems to have been strong-willed and intellectual. She taught all her children until they were nine or ten years old. Since tutors no doubt could have taught many subjects to the children, it is likely that Ann wanted to instill her love of literature and learning into a branch of the family in which money and possessions were of great importance.

If events had gone according to expectations, Robert Chapman would have entered adulthood as a gentleman, not having to earn a living. He could have devoted himself entirely to intellectual pursuits, the fine arts, or other tasks generally undertaken or overseen by the upper classes, as many of his forebears had done. God, however, had other plans for him.

Robert, a precocious child, often said that he wanted to become a poet. That desire revealed itself later in his hymn writing and in the style of his prose. He read constantly and was considered by many in his family to be far too bookish. When he was about ten years old, his parents secured a Roman Catholic priest from France to tutor him, probably in languages and literature. The tutor seems to have been a worthy instructor, if we can judge by the results. The fact that Robert's parents were willing to expose him to a Roman Catholic priest for one or two years is good evidence that they had no strong convictions about any particular branch of Christianity. Perhaps the priest discussed religion with his student, because when Robert left home at fifteen, he had a strong desire to find out what the Bible said. Although religion seems not to have been paramount in his immediate family, Anglican, Roman Catholic, and Quaker attitudes all influenced Robert's early life.

Robert was devoted to his mother and later said that when he was very young he cared little for anyone else as long as she was near him. Perhaps his mother favored him. She confided to a friend, "Robert always has a passion, whether literature or the flute, and whatever he takes up, he pursues diligently." Other Chapmans castigated the studious youngster, saying, "Robert is such a philosopher.

He won't do much." It would have been impossible for him not to be affected by such declarations of inadequacy. No doubt they caused him to draw even closer to his mother and into his books, away from the family's material interests.

His diligence, earnestness, and passion to enter thoroughly into topics that interested him did not leave as he grew up. The maturing youth demonstrated remarkable ability in languages; he studied a language until he mastered it. English, Danish, and French came to him naturally because they were spoken in the Thomas Chapman household. Robert also became proficient in German and Italian, probably with his tutor's help. After his conversion to Christ he studied Hebrew and Greek so he could read the Bible in those languages. When he became interested in doing missionary work in Spain, he studied Spanish and Portuguese until he could speak them fluently.

Ann Chapman's hope that her love of literature would be passed on to her son was realized. During Robert's adult years his acquaintances often remarked on his great literary knowledge, even though he received no formal education in literature after his fifteenth birthday. Italian literature was a favorite of his. As an adult he rendered this beautiful free translation of a sonnet by Michelangelo, the great Italian painter and sculptor:

My life, a voyage o'er a tempestuous sea
In a frail bark, draws near the common end
Of all men. I, as others, must descend
Into the grave. What profit now to me
Pencil or chisel? Where the gain to be
In highest art a monarch? Can I bend
God's sin-avenging justice to befriend
My helpless soul that would of guilt be free?
Nor saints nor angels can my ransom give
From the two deaths that are before mine eyes—
The first at hand: the twain my righteous doom—
But on the cross, the sinner to receive,
God's Son spread out His hands. He hears my cries;
To Him I look and triumph o'er the tomb.

A Change in Circumstances

When Robert reached his early teens, his father's business faltered during the Napoleonic wars in which Denmark sided with France. As a result of his conflict with Britain, Napoleon ordered all the ports under his control to close their markets to Britain. Whether or not this decree directly caused the Chapman business failure is not known. Whatever the cause, Thomas Chapman lost a great deal of money and was forced to relinquish his business. The future in Denmark looked bleak for the family, so Thomas and Ann moved back to Yorkshire. Although Thomas was not impoverished, his family could no longer maintain its former standard of living. This fact played a decisive role in Robert's life.

Enrolled in a Yorkshire preparatory school, Robert demonstrated his gift for languages and his love of literature. Still wanting to become a poet, he dreamed of devoting his life to books, writing, and scholarly achievement. However the family fortunes were now only a fraction of what they had been, so Robert would have to give up his gentleman's life and earn his living. He showed little interest in the sea and none in merchandising. Enrollment in Oxford or Cambridge would have been a natural course for him, and he apparently could have been admitted. The family was well-connected and the Thomas Chapmans seem to have re-established their link with the Church of England, a prerequisite for admission at that time. Perhaps the family's previous Quaker connections were an obstacle. More likely the larger Chapman family preferred that he enter the legal profession instead of pursuing academic interests.

In any event Robert left home at age fifteen and traveled to London in 1818 to begin a five-year apprenticeship with an attorney. Leaving home at an early age to learn a trade or profession was not rare at that time. Robert was intellectually mature beyond his years and probably quite ready to leave home. Other Chapmans lived in and around London, so he would not be completely isolated from his family.

If he was disappointed with this career choice, it is not apparent. He plunged into his apprenticeship with characteristic enthusiasm and determined to become an independent attorney. Part of his training consisted of copying legal documents, a task that must have been especially tedious for him. Studying legal precedents, court cases, procedures, and all the other details required of a good lawyer occupied his time not only at the office but also in his room during the evenings. As a youth he had "slept with Homer under my pillow," but no longer could he spend long and enjoyable hours with his beloved Italian classics.

Perhaps it is not too surprising that spiritual concerns also began to occupy Robert's mind. He needed to know where he stood before God and he began to read and study the Bible. During the next few years he read it through three or four times even though he questioned its authenticity. Much later he wrote that he was regarded during those years as a blameless, religious, and devout young man. "Long before I was quickened by the Spirit of God, I was considered a very godly young man, and I took to reading the Bible to see if it was a true book." From friends and libraries he borrowed books written by religious skeptics, but he found them generally unsatisfactory.

In spite of required legal study and growing religious concerns, Robert had a reasonably active social life. By his late teens he had grown tall and had a deep, resonant voice. Family connections opened many doors for him. On weekends and holidays he often attended parties in London's fashionable West End. Witty and articulate, he had become popular. But his confident manner and engaging smile hid an uneasiness, an unrest of spirit. His pleasant social activities seemed empty. Years later he wrote, "Sick was I of the world, hating it as vexation of spirit, while yet I was unable and unwilling to cast it out."

God's Holy Spirit and the Bible would not let him go. He read and reread the Bible, judged it, tried to refuse its judgment of himself, and tried to put it aside. The Bible was speaking to his heart, but he found many of its truths confusing and difficult to understand: God's love and wrath, His rejection of sin and His invitation to man to enter into communion with Himself. Chapman did not want to give up his pleasant life for an uncertain call. "I hugged my chains. I would not—could not—hear the voice of Jesus....My cup was bitter with my guilt and the fruit of my doings." He was acutely aware of his great problems in attempting to establish his righteousness in God's eyes. Outwardly happy and at ease, the sensitive young man was in turmoil.

After his five years of legal apprenticeship Chapman became an attorney of the Court of Common Pleas and an attorney of the Court of the King's Bench. Three years after that, at age twenty-three, he inherited a small fortune and set up his own law practice on Throgmorton Street in the banking center of London. He was successful from the beginning. Older lawyers praised and encouraged him. A brilliant future in law lay ahead.

3

The Doorway to a New Life

I n *Choice Sayings,* a compilation of Robert Chapman's sayings, we read: "The titles given to the Church in Scripture bespeak heavenly unity, such as the body, the vine, the temple of God, a holy nation, a chosen generation, a royal priesthood. Such words set forth the Church of God as a witness for Him in the world; but the names which have been invented by men are names of sects, and declare our shame." Those who are acquainted with the Brethren movement, of which Chapman was a part after about 1832, would naturally assume that his words derived from his colleagues, for this sentiment was commonly expressed among them. But Chapman very likely developed this attitude many years before the new movement was underway, for when he was twenty years old he was brought to the Lord by an uncommon man who held this conviction. This man was James Harington Evans.

Evans had been ordained in the Anglican church

(Church of England) in 1809, following the wishes of his father who was also an Anglican clergyman. Only after his ordination did the younger Evans learn about the doctrine of justification by faith alone, which to him was a life-changing revelation that he eagerly accepted. After his conversion, Evans' sermons focused heavily on the theme of justification by faith, which brought him a great deal of trouble.

Although many in his congregation were being converted as a result of this new message, others—especially those belonging to the upper classes—were greatly offended. Evans' father expressed concern that his son had become a Calvinist. In a very tender letter written at the end of 1816, Evans responded to his father with these words: "As to John Calvin, I am no follower of his. I desire to follow One indeed whom John Calvin followed, but this is all. Oh! when will those days come, when party names, party distinctions, party separations shall cease?"

Evans' rector and, no doubt, his higher superiors became uncomfortable with their maverick curate. The Anglican church especially disliked *enthusiasm,* at that time a pejorative word often used to describe evangelicals. Evans' preaching had become indistinguishable from the preaching of many dissenters or nonconformists—the Methodists, Baptists, Congregationalists, and other groups that dissented from the views and practices of the Anglican church. He was told to conform or resign.

Evans, not yet thirty years old and not yet humble, was in no mood to accommodate. Refusing to go against his maturing convictions, he boldly spoke and wrote against the church's deviation from Scriptural doctrines. He particularly opposed the union of church and state and the lack of discipline within the church. He deplored the fact that many adult members of the Church of England, some in leadership positions, were claiming salvation because of their baptism as infants, although they were clearly unregenerate.

At the end of 1815 Harington resigned from his curacy. A few painful months followed, during which Evans and his wife reviewed their decision to leave the Anglican

24

church. Evans was by now quite conscious of his weakness—his pride. *Have I acted in pride?* he wondered. After spending much time in prayer and conferring with others who had left the Anglican church, Evans and his wife knew they had acted correctly. He once again began preaching, this time in villages in western England. His friends recognized his remarkable preaching gift and advised him to exercise his ministry in London, which he did at the end of 1816. Soon the hall he was using overflowed with eager listeners.

After a few months he attracted the attention of wealthy Henry Drummond, a member of Parliament. Drummond, a nonconformist, was not strongly attached to any one group and was financially supportive of nonconformist causes. He often went to hear Evans preach and soon offered to build a new chapel where Evans would be free to preach and teach according to his own convictions. Thus John Street Chapel was built near the center of London in 1818, about the same time that Robert Chapman began his legal apprenticeship.

The new congregation at John Street was not affiliated with any existing Christian denomination or organization. As a result of Evans' powerful preaching, which spoke to the people's spiritual needs, the church grew rapidly. The attitude at John Street was one of openness; all believers as well as inquirers were welcomed.

ROBERT CHAPMAN MEETS CHRIST

One of the deacons at John Street Chapel, John Whitmore, was a lawyer. He was acquainted with twenty-year-old Chapman, who seemed quite pious, liked to speak of religious things, and seemed to know his Bible but spoke judgmentally of it. Whitmore soon realized that Chapman was searching for spiritual answers and had not found them. So Whitmore invited him to John Street Chapel to hear Harington Evans. With his upperclass upbringing, Chapman may have been reluctant to go at first, having heard much about the "enthusiasm" common in the dissenting churches. But he was searching for answers to his soul's unanswered longing and consented.

Chapman didn't know quite what to expect when he and Whitmore approached John Street Chapel that Sunday evening in 1823. People filing into the chapel came from many walks of life and the service was conducted with dignity by a man of evident culture who expressed every confidence in what he said. Here Chapman heard for the first time a sermon that opened the eyes of his heart. Never before had justification by faith and the atoning work of Christ been so clearly stated to him. As Evans preached, Chapman's intellectual reservations melted under the convicting power of the Holy Spirit. He accepted Christ as God's Son and as the One who had taken his own sins upon Himself.

A new life now opened before Chapman. He began studying the Bible with a new understanding. After reviewing the New Testament accounts of baptism he desired to be baptized at once. Evans advised him to wait until he more fully understood its significance, but with characteristic determination Chapman insisted on following the Lord's request as soon as possible. Wisely Harington Evans yielded, and a few days after being converted Chapman witnessed to Christ's working by being publicly baptized.

Chapman then told his family and friends about his conversion, but they could not understand its significance. "What! Robert converted? He didn't need converting!" one family member said. They hoped that Robert would not abandon his law profession and initially they were not disappointed. He continued in law and was quite successful, but he showed no sign of putting away his newfound love in Christ. Chapman did not have to convince his family of the reality of his faith; they could see it. When they realized that he would not turn back from his zealous devotion to the Bible and his conviction that it was God's Word, many of his relatives dismissed him from their circle. Later, looking back over those years, he wrote, "I became an offense to those I forsook, even those of my own flesh and blood."

The estrangement did not encompass the whole family however. One family member recorded that during this period Robert Chapman spent his vacation at the seaside with them, urging young relatives to study their Bibles. A few years after his conversion he drew close to a cousin and her husband, as we will see later. He remained close to his mother and later in life had good contact with brothers and sisters, some of whom also became converted.

As a result of his decision to follow Christ, Chapman also faced rejection from casual acquaintances who were offended and convicted by his enthusiasm for the Savior. The following story, which Chapman related, reveals not only his prayer life but also the confidence he had in his Father's care:

> Shortly after my conversion a great and unforeseen trial suddenly fell upon me. A certain person took it into his mind to oppose and persecute me in every possible manner. I was puzzled by it, for I had nothing but love in my heart for him; but what did I? Just gave myself and the trial right over to God, and left it with Him; and I had the joy also of making repeated intercession for my opposer. What was the outcome? In time the blessed Lord brought salvation to him and unto his family.

Young Chapman took Christianity seriously. Many years later he wrote:

> I remember the time when I was afraid to die.... But on coming to Christ and being saved by Him, I passed from that state to another, that of being afraid to live, for I feared that if I lived I might do something that would dishonor the Lord, and I would rather die a hundred times than do such a thing. But thanks be to God, I did not remain long in this state, for I saw clearly that it was possible to live in the world without dishonoring God.

This statement reflects Jesus' prayer for His disciples,

as recorded in the Gospel of John: "I do not ask Thee to take them out of the world, but to keep them from the evil one" (John 17:15, NASB). Chapman learned that the Christian should live and work and witness in this world; since the Father answered the Son's prayer, the Christian should understand that although he is within Satan's reach, he is not within Satan's grasp.

GROWING HUNGER FOR GOD'S WORD

In 1823 Chapman completed his apprenticeship and became a solicitor. His first employer was Freshfields, one of the leading firms of solicitors in England. Chapman worked hard at his new profession. His intelligence and dedication attracted the attention of the more experienced men of the court and they gave him considerable encouragement. After three years he inherited a small fortune and decided to use these funds to set up a private practice. His new firm thrived; his gracious manner of dealing with people and his cultured upbringing served him well.

Chapman began attending the weekly communion service at John Street Chapel on Sunday evenings. Not many members of the congregation did this; most preferred to attend the more formal monthly communion service held on a Sunday morning. Little is known of how Harington Evans conducted this evening service; we do not know who served the elements and whether the meeting was open to any believer who wished to contribute in prayer or a brief word. But if Chapman's subsequent style for these remembrance meetings is a reflection of Evans'—and it probably is—the meeting must have encouraged open participation. Chapman loved this time in which people worshiped God from their hearts. It was a time of prayer, worship, and remembrance of Christ's work at Calvary—a type of meeting different from preaching and teaching services. When Chapman established his own ministry a few years later, he always stressed the importance of this type of meeting for all believers.

Under Evans' encouragement Chapman became involved in the ministry at John Street Chapel. Evans recognized in Chapman a true servant's heart and spent a great deal of time with him. Without any training in preaching apart from what Evans provided, Chapman began speaking at various services at John Street Chapel. His first attempts consisted of carefully constructed and sometimes convoluted arguments typical of a lawyer presenting his case before a jury. After a while he realized that this type of preaching was not very helpful to most listeners. They needed encouragement and a demonstration of concern as well as doctrinal instruction, and it all needed to be presented simply. This was what Evans was giving them.

After hearing his first sermons some of Chapman's friends offered the opinion that he would never be a good preacher. This undoubtedly caused him a lot of anguish, and his reply was telling: "There are many who preach Christ, but not so many who live Christ. My great aim will be to *live* Christ." This became his goal: to love Christ, to love and care for the poor, and to carry God's message of salvation. Chapman gradually developed his own style of preaching with Evans' help and was recognized later as a good preacher. He had one quite remarkable natural gift: his voice. It was deep and resonant, and throughout his life many people remarked on it. Through the years he learned to use it with great effect in public reading as well as preaching.

An incident that occurred during this period shows how Chapman's knowledge of the Bible was growing. Two clients of his were in conflict; one had decided to sue the other, and the second was going to contest the suit in court. After consulting with them Chapman realized that both were professing Christians, so he promptly brought them together in his office and turned his Bible to 1 Corinthians 6. He explained what they evidently did not know: that members of Christ's body should resolve conflicts among themselves within the confines of that body. Chapman convinced his clients that they needed to obey the Scriptures and they both withdrew their suits. Thus began Chapman's career of counseling Christians. He did not hesitate to give advice during counseling sessions, but he always gave it in a gentle spirit and based it on what he saw in the Scriptures. Obedience to the Scriptures was paramount to him.

The literature that once had so delighted him lost much of its appeal. His main reading interest was now the Bible. It was God's message to him, the book that gave meaning to his life. During these years he studied Hebrew and Greek in order to read the Bible in its original languages. He no longer needed to spend his evenings studying law, and Bible study now occupied his time. As this happened, his interest in law began to wane. Earthly ambition gave way to heavenly, and he developed an expanding desire to tell people of Christ's love for them.

His old friends gradually left him. His very life had become an indictment to many of them and it was not long before Robert was socially isolated from them. This did not greatly concern him, however, for he had made new friends at John Street Chapel. These friends, many from poor backgrounds quite different from his own, were loving and shared his spirit. With them he entered into a completely new life, one devoted to concern with the spiritual welfare of people, especially poor people. Robert Chapman was becoming an evangelist with a strong social concern.

John Street Chapel lay near a district of tenements where poverty ran deep and the dwellers lived without much hope of a better life. It was the area Charles Dickens described so graphically a few years later. Chapman developed a concern for the welfare of these people. He wanted to learn how they lived and what they thought, but he soon realized that his life of relative luxury and comforts stood in sharp contrast to theirs. His lifestyle became an indictment and a burden to him. Gradually his interest in these people changed from an intellectual compassion to an identification with them. He started bringing them food and clothing rather than having the assistance delivered. He spent time with them and told them about Christ's love, which they could understand because of the love he showed to them. He took a particular interest, for example, in a poor old blind woman. He brought her to the chapel each Sunday and afterward saw her safely to her dwelling again. The number brought to the Lord by his ministry during those years must have been large.

Evans' influence on Chapman's life and attitudes toward Christian worship was profound. Chapman's confidence in the all-sufficiency of the Bible, his devotedness to a weekly observance of the Lord's Supper, his emphasis on believer's baptism (although not insisting on it as a condition of membership or fellowship), and his views on the unity of all Christians—earmarks of his subsequent ministry—were the same as Evans'.

For some time Chapman continued in both his legal profession and his work at John Street Chapel. But as time went on he realized that his heart was not in his law practice. His greatest interest was in telling people about the Lord and he spent many of his evenings visiting those who lived in the slums near the chapel. He became deeply concerned about whether he should leave his profession and his successful practice. As is common with people whose hearts are ready, God soon showed him his next role in life.

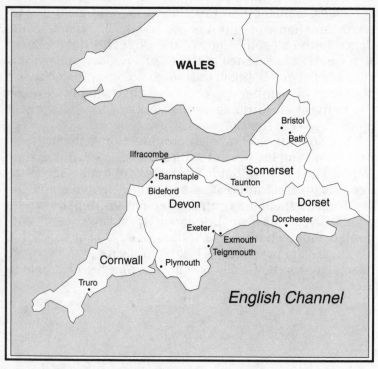

Barnstaple and the surrounding towns in Devon where Chapman spent most of his years.

4
A Developing Work in Devon

As Robert Chapman's involvement in John Street Chapel grew, God was at work in the hearts of many people, bringing about a renewal of His church. Let's briefly look at some of these people and the developing work in southwestern England, for Chapman was soon to be in the center of this activity.

Not all of Robert's family had distanced themselves from him, and his first cousin Susan was one of those who had not. In 1823 she married a wealthy west-country lawyer, Thomas Pugsley, who was a member of a prominent family long associated with Devonshire, a county on the south side of the Bristol channel in western England. Thomas and his bride made their home in the beautiful countryside near the market town of Barnstaple, which was a commercial center for the northern part of Devon.

When Susan heard through family circles that Robert had experienced a spiritual conversion, she wanted to hear more. She and Thomas sought him out when they next took the two-day trip by horse-drawn carriage from Barnstaple to London. Both were interested in knowing the particulars of his conversion and what it signified. Chapman responded to their interest enthusiastically. The three began studying the Bible together and praying. During one of their visits the Pugsleys put their trust in Christ. Although Chapman later referred to Thomas as "a child of mine in the faith," Thomas strongly influenced Robert as well.

When the Pugsleys observed Chapman's expanding work with poor people in London, they decided to become similarly involved and minister to the poor in the Barnstaple area. Workhouses in those days were places where people who had no hope of employment and no one to care for them were fed, clothed, and housed. In return they were expected to perform some type of menial labor. Thomas decided to set up gospel meetings each Sunday at the workhouse in Pilton, a small village bordering Barnstaple on the north. When word of these meetings at the workhouse got around, people from the neighborhood began coming to them.

As their work grew, the Pugsleys became convinced that evangelizing the lower classes was the Lord's calling for them. So about 1829 Thomas took a courageous step. He decided to relinquish his profession and devote all his time to the Lord's work. He and Susan moved to Tawstock, a small hamlet three miles southwest of Barnstaple. There they became actively involved in the leadership of several small churches, some of which met in people's homes.

A short time before this, Thomas became associated with a local evangelist named Robert Gribble, who later worked with Chapman. In contrast to Pugsley, Gribble was born into a poor family and received a minimal education. He started his own drapery business, which became substantial enough to support his growing family. Sometime during this period he experienced a spiritual conversion and began teaching in the afternoon Sunday school at the Congregational Church in Barnstaple. The fruit of this effort was so rewarding that in 1815 Gribble began setting up Sunday schools in several nearby villages.

Soon parents of the children asked Gribble to preach on Sunday evenings to adults. After initial hesitancy, Gribble consented and discovered his real gift. In only two years his knowledge of the Bible and his developing ability in public speaking enabled him to preach regularly in various schools and churches. His common speech, far from being a hindrance, was quite useful; the villagers responded enthusiastically to him, and many turned to the Lord.

Several house churches or cottage meetings started in the region around Barnstaple as a result of Gribble's work. The Congregational denomination, also called the Independents, built Tawstock Chapel for some of the believers in 1817 and asked Gribble to become its pastor. A few years later Lovacott Chapel was built just a few miles away and Gribble oversaw its spiritual welfare as well. In addition to performing his pastoral duties, he evangelized constantly throughout the countryside.

During this time Gribble kept his drapery business going as his means of support, perhaps modeling himself after the apostle Paul. However Gribble devoted less and less attention to his business and eventually it failed. He took this as evidence of a personal weakness and, against the wishes of the congregation at Tawstock Chapel, resigned his pastorate. Probably feeling that he needed to align himself more closely with the Independent denomination, he decided to join their home missionary station. Thomas Pugsley, who by then was working with and accepted by the people around Tawstock, took Gribble's place.

In 1829 Gribble moved his family away from Barnstaple to the missionary station in South Devon near the city of Exeter. The Lord was behind this move because on the first day of his new work, Gribble met William Hake, who would play an important role not only in his life but also in the life of Chapman and several others in our story. Gribble had until then been satisfied with just preaching a simple gospel message. This had been a fruitful style of ministry for him; many people had been converted and several had become missionaries. But he had paid relatively little attention to Biblical doctrines apart from salvation and had accepted Congregationalist traditions without much consideration. Hake began challenging him on subjects ranging from the theological (such as the meaning of baptism because the Independents practiced infant baptism) to the practical (such as the propriety of pew rents, which were then commonly used to pay the salary of the pastor). Gribble later wrote, "This was a new thing to me, having been accustomed, as many I fear still are, to receive what I had been taught, without taking the pains to examine whether it was in accordance with the Scriptures, the only infallible standard of truth."

Not long afterward Gribble changed his views on those subjects. He became dissatisfied with the missionary station—not just for doctrinal reasons. "Some of the members of the association were men of the world, not even professing to be Christians, yet they had a voice in all the measures adopted." He did not keep his discontent to himself, and in his third year there he was asked to withdraw from the station. Old friends asked him to return to North Devon to continue his evangelistic work, and in March 1832 he returned with his family. Penniless, but confident that the Lord would provide for all his needs, he conducted a fruitful ministry until nearly the end of his life in the 1860s.

Thomas Pugsley, through his work at Tawstock Chapel, became acquainted with William Hake about this time, very likely through Robert Gribble. And in 1830 Hake most likely introduced Pugsley to an enthusiastic young German, George Müller, who had recently arrived in England and was eager to preach. The ministry was growing, so in 1830 Pugsley, with his own funds, built yet another chapel in nearby Hiscot. Obviously impressed by George Müller, Pugsley invited him to preach the first sermon at the Hiscot Chapel.

These men—Pugsley, Gribble, Hake, and Müller—along with Henry Craik and Elizabeth Paget were instrumental in the renewed spread of the gospel in southwestern England and would soon become coworkers with Chapman. (See appendix B.)

5

The Invitation to Barnstaple

In the summer of 1831 the Pugsleys invited Robert Chapman to spend his vacation with them and help out in their evangelistic work. Chapman, who enjoyed the company of his cousin and loved the beautiful country of North Devon, gladly accepted the invitation. Shortly after Chapman arrived, Pugsley suggested that he preach weekly at the Pilton workhouse and Robert readily agreed.

A broad-shouldered, twenty-nine-year-old lawyer from London who was tall, cultured, and could also preach, immediately attracted attention. One Sunday evening a group of girls came to the workhouse to see him preach. (They were probably not too interested in what he had to say.) But what they saw was not so important as what they heard, and what happened that evening was not what they had expected. They heard a sermon on sin and its consequences. One girl, Eliza Gilbert, said afterward of Chapman's sermon, "He hurt me. I must hear him again."

She did and shortly after that she accepted Christ. Later she became an important part of Chapman's ministry.

It is quite certain that the Pugsleys had more in mind for Chapman than relaxation and weekly preaching because they invited William Hake of Exeter to visit them while Robert was there. Chapman reminded them of Hake, although Hake was a few years older and married. Both men had a similar temperament, were fervent students of the Bible, and were completely devoted to Christ. Susan and Thomas also knew that Hake had an interesting story to tell.

At the time of their meeting, Hake was running a boarding school for boys in a large house that was the former residence of Anthony Norris Groves. Groves' devout life had enormously impacted many lives. Born in 1795, Groves was a longtime friend of Hake. He had been a dentist with a thriving business in Exeter, but eventually his wealth began making him uncomfortable. After much prayer and contemplation, he and his wife Mary agreed that they should spend the rest of their lives spreading the gospel as missionaries and that they would live in complete dependence on God's provision. In 1825 Groves wrote and published his convictions in a pamphlet, *Christian Devotedness,* which became widely known. He was at that time a loyal member of the Church of England, but a series of incidents caused him to break with it.

Although he no longer had the support of the Anglican church, Groves' desire for missionary work intensified. He and Mary then took an unusual step. In spite of a complete lack of organizational backing, they sold all their possessions and gave away most of their money, keeping only enough to finance their missionary journey. They chose to go to Baghdad, the city to which they felt God was calling them, and they determined to rely entirely on God's provision for the continuance of this work. They turned their house over to William Hake for the purpose of establishing a Christian boarding school, gave the dental practice to a nephew, distributed their assets, and (accompanied by their children and a few others) left the country to devote their lives to missionary service.

This story must have profoundly impacted Chapman, as it had many others. Upon returning to London and his law practice, Chapman was quite uncertain that he wanted to continue in his profession. His experience in the Barnstaple area had produced an exhilaration that he had not previously felt. He began to wonder if God would have him leave his practice, renounce worldly possessions, and devote himself to fulltime Christian service. Being a pastor in the manner of Evans and Pugsley was attractive to him, but he also entertained the idea of becoming a missionary to Spain or Italy.

Then Chapman received an invitation, probably through the influence of Pugsley, to pastor Ebenezer Chapel in Barnstaple, a troubled and leaderless congregation of Particular Baptists. Ebenezer Chapel seems to have been divided into two factions. A majority agreed with the invitation and were open to change if Chapman wanted it; a divisive minority was opposed to change. Going from a dynamic church such as John Street Chapel to a moribund one is generally not a happy prospect, but Chapman felt that the hand of God was in the invitation. However, he knew he could not be a conventional Particular Baptist pastor.

A distinctive of the Particular Baptists was their insistence that only those who had been baptized as believers should be allowed to participate in communion and admitted to membership. Not only was Chapman uncomfortable with denominational boundaries; he did not share Particular Baptist views on baptism. His only alternative was to tell them his beliefs plainly, which he did. He also told the congregation that he would come only on the condition that he could teach whatever he found in the Scriptures.

The Ebenezer Chapel congregation at once accepted his conditions. This shows that they were a church in disarray. In fact during the preceding eighteen months Ebenezer Chapel had been served by three pastors; four had served during the nine years since the chapel was built. Some people in that congregation were obviously making the situation difficult for their pastors, yet did not want to assume leadership responsibilities within the church.

Chapman surely knew that the congregation was not unified and that a new leader would have difficulties guiding two groups with differing attitudes. Knowing these problems and planning an ambitious program of visitation, he began thinking about the merits of shared leadership. He contacted his new acquaintance, William Hake, and invited him to share in the ministry at Ebenezer. Hake was not able to join him at that time, but did join Chapman many years later.

Chapman knew the situation, yet he came, leaving behind all prospects of earthly advancement. He must have been utterly convinced of God's call to that work because he gave away his private fortune and his inheritances, keeping only enough to purchase a house in Barnstaple and sustain himself initially. In April 1832 he left his successful law practice, his beloved John Street Chapel, his friend and mentor Harington Evans, and all the attractions of London and moved to Barnstaple.

A City in Spiritual Bondage

The town to which Robert Chapman came had a long history. Established in A.D. 930, the ancient town was strategically situated, lying at the junction of the rivers Taw and Yeo and accessible by ship from the sea. When the Normans seized the small community from the Saxons, they built a high stone wall around it, threw up a fifty-foot-high mound of dirt within it, and erected a wooden castle on the mound. The mound still stands, but the castle and wall are gone.

When Chapman arrived in 1832 to begin what was to become his life's work, Barnstaple was a bustling town of about seven thousand people. Surrounded by many small villages and in a valley almost at sea level, it was both a farming market and seaport. Large vessels plied the estuary of the Taw river. The town was an active export and import center for merchants dealing in wool, sheep, cattle, and produce. It also boasted a hospital, a prison, a daily newspaper, two or three hotels, a number of smaller inns, and a multitude of drinking establishments.

The Taw river flows north down from the hilly country toward Barnstaple, but when it reaches the town it abruptly turns west and moves leisurely to the sea as a broad estuary. The small Yeo river, whose waters come from the hills to the east, joins the Taw at the bend. The villages on the west side of the Taw could be reached from Barnstaple only by a single bridge or by boat. To the north the land rises more steeply and ends abruptly at the Bristol channel some ten miles away. Sheep and cattle graze the green rolling hillsides around Barnstaple.

The town was in the shape of a teardrop with its point on the south. The two rivers formed the west and north boundaries of Barnstaple. Boutport Street—so named because it went 'bout the port—struck southward from the Yeo river, followed the site of the ancient wall on the east side of the town, and curved to meet the Taw river at the point of the teardrop. The street more or less defined Barnstaple's eastern edge during the early nineteenth century, although some industry, along with housing for its workers, had developed on the east side. From west to east, the town was little more than a quarter mile wide at its widest point.

Bear Street was the main road leaving Barnstaple to points east. A causeway over the Yeo river permitted an easy walk to the village of Pilton, which bordered Barnstaple on the north. At the southern edge of Barnstaple lay Newport village, separated from the larger town by a marshy area. Farther south on the hillside was Bishop's Tawton, and on the west side of the Taw river lay Tawstock and several other tiny hamlets.

Barnstaple itself, although located in an area of great natural beauty close by the moors of North Devon and close by the sea, was not attractive in those days. It had been built on marshy ground and drainage had long been a problem. Pens for the animals brought to market were located in the middle of town. A yard for tanning animal hides was in the Derby area to the east of Boutport Street;

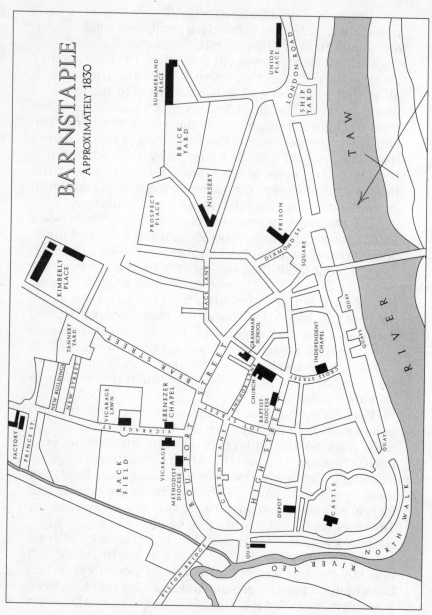

A map of Barnstaple at the time Chapman arrived.

An aerial view of Barnstaple around 1930.
(photo courtesy of R. L. Knight)

The town square of Barnstaple in 1897. The square is where many of the fairs and other public events were held.

its odors seemed to define the character of Derby. A noisy, dusty limekiln worked on the riverfront at the southern edge of Barnstaple. The streets were narrow and dirty, and many of the townspeople lived in great poverty, although people of considerable wealth also lived there and in the surrounding neighborhood. Alcohol was a great evil in the town. Its inhabitants supported eighty "licensed houses," which sold liquor and were permitted to remain open through the night. Beer houses were even more common. Drinking seemed to be the only outlet of many of the poor and it trapped them in their condition.

Ebenezer Chapel was located on Vicarage Lane, a small street that began at Boutport Street and ran eastward, parallel to Bear Street and a block north of it. The chapel consisted of a modest brick building almost across the street from the Anglican vicar's quarters and about a hundred steps from Boutport Street. To the east of the chapel

Left, a view down Vicarage Street in the late 1800s. *(photo courtesy of North Devon Athenaeum)*

Right, Ebenezer Chapel, located on Vicarage Street, as it looks today.
(photo courtesy of the author)

was the Derby area where many of the poorer people lived. Many of them worked at the tanyard or at a lace factory another quarter-mile farther out. Derby was known for its cramped housing, dark alleyways, poverty, and barefoot children who wore rags and played in the streets. Fights and drunken brawls were frequent. The police preferred to walk in pairs when they patrolled the district.

Yet Barnstaple's spiritual condition was probably not much worse—or better—than other English towns its size. Several dissenting churches and an Anglican parish church were there, but they had not reached the poverty-stricken people in a significant way. The Wesleyan and Whitefield revivals of the preceding century were now two generations in the past. Robert Gribble, Thomas Pugsley, and others had evangelized in the area for several years prior to Chapman's arrival, but their impact was not yet substantial.

A Man Possessing Godly Vision

Chapman had chosen his course before he came. His goals extended far beyond pastoring Ebenezer Chapel. He had already decided to make the entire town his parish. The pockets of poverty reminded him of the London slums and his heart went out to their residents. But he had yet another goal. In London he had seen and heard about many missionaries and preachers who had become weary and discouraged from overwork, yet had no place to flee to for rest and temporary relief from their responsibilities. Chapman wanted to make his home a resting place for such missionaries and other servants of the Lord. Like Barnabas of the New Testament, Chapman had a gift of encouragement. If he could pray with these workers, talk to them, listen to them, and provide them with a retreat, perhaps they could return to their tasks with renewed enthusiasm.

Chapman first rented rooms in a small house on Gammon Lane near the town center, but at once began looking for a suitable house to buy—larger than he would need for himself and located in a poor section of town. He found his ideal home in the Derby area. Part of a rowhouse that extended the length of New Buildings Street, it was close to Ebenezer Chapel—and it had room for guests. His new home was at No. 6 New Buildings Street, a narrow lane just 150 feet long, running south off Vicarage Lane, but blocked from entrance to Bear Street by the tanyard. The funds to buy the house probably came from money he had set aside for that purpose when he gave away his private fortune. No. 6 New Buildings Street had been designed for a family with children. With a gabled room above the second floor, it suited him well. Chapman lived there for the next seventy years. A friend once offered him the use of a large comfortable house in a better section of Barnstaple, but Chapman declined. He wanted to live where even the poorest person could come to him without hesitation.

As Chapman prepared and furnished the house, he sent word to those he knew in London, Devon, and elsewhere that any missionary or other type of Christian worker would be welcome to stay without cost at his dwelling for as long as he or she wished. As for the funds to maintain this enterprise, he believed that the Lord would see to that. This was to be a faith ministry and Chapman believed that those who came to rest for a while could be taught a valuable lesson even in this.

Almost as soon as he moved to Barnstaple, Chapman began his tireless work of visitation and evangelization. He talked with people on the streets and at their houses or rooms. He frequently held gospel meetings in the workhouses and talked individually with the homeless and destitute inmates. He often walked great distances to visit and preach in the small villages near Barnstaple, sometimes teaming up with Gribble and Pugsley.

Soon Chapman became well known in town. He began open-air preaching during this early period and became quite good at it. In Barnstaple he generally preached in the town square, the site of the clock tower. Sometimes he moved across the road and preached on the broad strand of the Taw river. He used his height and deep voice with great effect in preaching and many people came to know

Right, one side of the short street called New Buildings. The woman is standing outside the door of #6—the home of Robert Chapman.

Above, Robert Chapman's workshop where he liked to work alone, usually making gifts for his guests.

Left, Chapman's bedroom. Notice the books on the mantle—mostly Bibles in various languages.

the Lord. Chapman did not wait for organizational backing before beginning his work of visitation and preaching out-of-doors; it was not a requirement of his pastorate at Ebenezer. He knew that God had called him to do this kind of work and he did it for the rest of his life.

Many people today are offended by the preaching of the gospel in public places. They would prefer that such preaching be confined to a church building. But much of Jesus' ministry took place in the open, where the people were, and this is no doubt why Chapman placed such importance on it. With a few exceptions, Chapman generally had little trouble with crowds when he preached in the open. He preached with dignity and sensitivity, and most people respected him. Many years later a woman related this story, which shows how well he was accepted:

> While I was living in a situation in the country, Mr. Chapman came to preach in our village. He stood all alone, and people were gathering around him. My master and I stood by the door listening for a little while, and suddenly I thought I would go and get a chair for him to stand upon. My master, observing my movements, said, "What are you going to do, Mary?"
>
> I replied, "Going to get a chair for that dear, blessed young man to stand upon," for most blessed truth was pouring out of his mouth.
>
> He said, "Get the very best you can find, Mary."

It may be difficult for many of us to identify with Chapman. A man of culture and high intelligence from a family of wealth and influence, he now poured himself into the hearts and souls of poor and ignorant people. Having built a successful career and developed stimulating friendships, and being accustomed to the comforts of life, he now ate the food and shared the discomforts of the poverty-stricken. Even some of his colleagues in the work felt that he had gone to unnecessary, even senseless, extremes. But the imitation of Christ was Chapman's chosen way of life.

An open-air service with Robert Chapman preaching.
(Chapman is the white-bearded man in the top
right-hand corner of the photo.)

6
Early Days at Ebenezer Chapel

Chapman's objectives at Ebenezer Chapel quickly became evident. To Chapman, the Bible sufficiently addressed all matters of life and was life's only reliable book. He taught simply and only from the Bible because he was convinced that most churchgoers really knew little about what it contained. Believing that too much emphasis had been placed on denominational tradition and not enough on genuine searching of the Scriptures, he felt that believers should have a fuller appreciation of what Christ's death on the cross meant in their personal lives.

CHANGES IN SUNDAY WORSHIP

Communion

Chapman changed both the style and frequency of the communion observance at Ebenezer. He felt it desirable to celebrate the Lord's Supper, as communion was usually called, each Sunday in the manner he had learned at

John Street Chapel. He wanted the observance to be not a solemn ritual, but a worship service in which all members of the church could openly participate as they felt led by the Holy Spirit. Someone would suggest singing a hymn; one of the men might speak briefly on a portion of Scripture; then perhaps the congregation would sing another hymn; another man would pray; and so forth as people felt led. The bread and cup would then be taken, passed hand to hand. Chapman or another recognized teacher who might be present would then teach from the Scriptures. This would be a single service, lasting perhaps two hours. Chapman never asserted that a definite pattern for the Lord's Supper was decreed in Scripture. He did, however, insist that the service be focused on the cross and that it should not be considered a rite that provided saving grace to the participants.

Baptism

Although Chapman had firm convictions on the importance of baptism after conversion, he shared Harington Evans' belief that baptism was not a criterion for membership or participation in communion. He taught that all believers, by profession of faith and life, were not merely free to participate, but were invited to by Christ Jesus Himself, and this applied whether His followers had been baptized as believers or not.

Wisely Chapman did not insist on rapid change in any matter. Although he preached a different message, for a time he allowed the Ebenezer tradition to continue: the unbaptized were not permitted to participate in the Lord's Supper. This was a sensitive issue, and not just among Particular Baptists. Believers coming out of the Church of England or the Congregational churches, which had a long tradition of infant baptism, found the notion of baptism as a requirement for membership difficult to accept. Chapman understood this problem and although he desired that all Christians be baptized following conversion as an act of obedience and public witness, he did not insist on it for other believers. Minds do change, but slowly as a rule.

After about a year nearly all the members of Ebenezer agreed to this position and it was adopted by the church.

Chapman said later that Christian leaders in the south of Devon who learned of his work at Ebenezer and felt a kinship with him, advised him to insist at once on the abandonment of this Particular Baptist tradition. So he had to overcome pressure from this direction also. Some people are resistant to change; some want change at once. Every Christian leader experiences this dilemma at some time. Chapman's way of handling this situation reveals his patience, gentle instruction, and waiting on the Lord. He knew that unless a great majority of the church supported a decision affecting a longstanding tradition, great disaffection and disunity would result. He said later, "We waited in patience for fulness of unity of judgment....What we now enjoy here of mutual love and the Spirit's unity would never have been our portion had any other course been taken."

Music

Chapman also changed the congregational singing at Ebenezer. To him, an ideal hymn should lead one through the cross of Christ to God Himself. He believed there were not enough of such hymns, a belief he probably developed at John Street Chapel in London, where it is likely he composed some hymns. In any case, he set out soon after he arrived to develop a new collection of hymns. By 1837 he had written enough to publish a new hymnbook that the Christians under Chapman's leadership used for many years.

A hymn writer's experiences and longings find expression in the hymns he or she writes. The themes running through most of Chapman's hymns were the sufferings of Christ and the glories that should follow. A verse from one of his hymns expresses his well-known thirst for a greater knowledge of the love of Christ:

> I would, my Lord and Saviour,
> Know that which no measure knows;

Would search the mystery of Thy love,
The depth of all Thy woes.

One of Chapman's best-known hymns begins:

O my Saviour crucified!
Near Thy cross would I abide;
There to look, with steadfast eye,
On thy dying agony.

This is typical of Chapman's emphasis on the cross of Calvary, asking for our response of love and devotion to Christ, who took our sins upon Himself.

Chapman's sister Arabella once remarked that only those who knew him could fully appreciate his hymns, for they alone knew how fully his life corresponded to them. His emphasis on the sufferings of Christ may be a reflection of his anguish as through the years he watched Christians strive with one another, divide, and generally act in un-Christlike ways. But we should remember that Chapman was convinced that only by returning in spirit to Calvary and reflecting on Christ's dying love for sinners can a Christian develop and maintain proper perspective toward the world and toward Christ. Hymns are one of the more powerful ways to express such truths.

SPIRITUAL CHANGES IN MANY LIVES

Chapman's preaching and teaching also emphasized obedience to God's Word in conduct and attitudes and obedience in telling others of Christ's love for them. Attracted by this emphasis on the Bible as well as by the example of Chapman's life, new people began attending and joining Ebenezer Chapel. Ebenezer grew rapidly in numbers and in spirituality during those earliest years, and a number of people met Christ. Let's look at a few examples of how God used Chapman to bring Christ's joy and hope into several people's lives, who then shared the gospel with others.

Eliza Gilbert

Eliza, who had been converted under Chapman's preaching at the Pilton workhouse in 1831, became a faithful member of Ebenezer Chapel. She told Chapman that she wanted to be baptized but her unconverted mother was so opposed to the idea that she had threatened to make Eliza leave home if she insisted on it. Eliza nevertheless wanted to go through with it and the baptism took place. Many at Ebenezer Chapel were quite anxious for her and followed her home after the baptism. True to her word, the mother refused to let Eliza into the house, so friends let her stay with them during this trying period. After a few months Eliza became very ill and the doctors thought she would die. Her mother, on hearing this, relented and permitted Eliza to return home, but would not speak to her.

Once a week Robert Chapman was permitted to visit Eliza, and the mother would leave during these times. Eliza was also permitted to receive letters from him, and three of them have been preserved. These are the oldest existing Chapman letters and they date from 1835. In them he wrote words of encouragement and compassion to Eliza, reminding her of God's hand in all things and telling her that she should look to the Lord for help and strength. Although Eliza's initial interest in Chapman at Pilton, her faithful attendance at Ebenezer, her coming to him about baptism, and his constant attention to her during her illness would seem to suggest a mutual attraction, there is no trace of any romantic involvement between them. In fact Chapman never married.

Eliza eventually recovered from her illness and became a stalwart of the congregation. Other members of her family were eventually converted through her influence and Chapman's ministry. Her mother also, in old age, finally yielded to Christ.

William Bowden and George Beer

Another early convert of Chapman, William Bowden was an energetic twenty-year-old who soon became an ardent evangelist and worked with Chapman among the poor of Barnstaple. Yet another who was attracted to Ebenezer Chapel because of Chapman's ministry and example was George Beer, also about twenty years old. Uneducated and apprenticed to a farmer as a boy, he had been converted under Gribble's preaching. Beer and Bowden became good friends and often worked together, preaching and evangelizing in the villages around Barnstaple. Several small house churches were started in those hamlets as a result of their work and some of them grew large enough to require a building and adopt a regular schedule of meetings.

These congregations depended on Bowden, Beer, Chapman, and other willing leaders for pastoral care. Since Ebenezer was still nominally Baptist at that time, these small churches usually considered themselves to be Baptist, but they operated along lines similar to those at Ebenezer Chapel. Records that have been found of these churches and the earlier ones near Tawstock, Lovacott, and Hiscot often reveal an ambiguity about denominational affiliation. This is the result of Chapman's influence, who had become quite opposed to denominational distinctions. The Christians in those churches were all "Christian Brethren" to him, and several called themselves that after a time.

With Chapman's encouragement, Bowden and Beer began open-air preaching. When they did this in the Derby area, they were exposed to much abuse and continual threat of physical violence. But many people received Christ through their efforts, and this strengthened their conviction that God was calling them to a lifetime of evangelistic ministry.

The help Bowden and Beer provided Chapman did not last long however. In 1835 Anthony Groves returned to England. He had worked five years in Baghdad under incredible hardship. About a year after his arrival there, a plague killed half the population of the city in just two months, including his wife and infant daughter. That was followed soon by an enormous flood and a war between rival factions that took many more lives. Some who went with him, or who came later to help, returned to England disheartened. Five years of work had resulted in only a little fruit and much discouragement. But God commands His own to be faithful, not successful, and Groves determined to press on.

Hearing of an open door for missions work in India, he visited there and found that the door was open to the gospel; only a lack of workers hindered its spread. So Groves returned to England and the continent to recruit men and women willing to return to India with him. While abroad, Groves had corresponded frequently with many friends in southwestern England and Ireland; thus Chapman was quite aware of his activities, although he had not yet met him. When Groves came to Barnstaple at Chapman's invitation, he found that Bowden, Beer, and their wives were willing to go with him. God had prepared them and they were ready and eager to enter into their life's work. Chapman encouraged them and a few months later they left. They settled in the Godavari Delta of India and there laid the foundation for a strong Christian work.

The Rector's Daughter

The Wreys, part of a distinguished old family with the hereditary rank of baronet, lived near the Pugsleys in the Tawstock area. One of the Wreys, rector of the local parish, was on good terms with the Pugsleys. Through Thomas and Susan, Chapman was introduced to the Wreys shortly after his arrival in Barnstaple. Chapman's culture and bearing made him quite acceptable to them. Witnessing for Christ was so natural to Chapman that soon a daughter of the rector was converted. Not long after that, she declared her intention to be baptized. Her rejection of the significance of her baptism as an infant placed her father in a peculiar position. But he seems to have made no public resistance and plans for the baptism in the Taw river went forward.

Word of the upcoming event spread quickly and many curious townspeople came to see Chapman baptize the rector's daughter. But there was another unusual twist to the event: Chapman was going to baptize a young farmer at the same time. People from widely separated classes did not often participate in mutual activities at that time. The Wrey family, however, was not scandalized by the circumstances of their daughter's baptism. More likely the townspeople watched in wonder at the double spectacle before them in the Taw river. Chapman characteristically broke down barriers between classes in living out the common life in Christ.

Following his baptism, the young farmer, George Lovering, soon began evangelizing in that neighborhood. He worked for another thirty years in North Devon, establishing churches in several villages to the south and east of Barnstaple.

Chapman's first years at Ebenezer Chapel saw much spiritual fruit. Evangelism in Barnstaple and the countryside was the keynote of the revitalized chapel. But such successes seldom proceed without trials and Satan soon attempted to halt the Christians' testimony.

A baptism at the Taw river similar to many conducted by Chapman.

7

Tough Decisions; Godly Choices

Some members of Ebenezer Chapel's congregation never did agree to the changes urged by Chapman and adopted by the majority. Seeing that Ebenezer Chapel had changed course and was not likely to return to Particular Baptist traditions, they left as a group in 1834. The capable, gentle Chapman was not able to stop the defection. If the majority had not been so unified in spirit and purpose, the secession could easily have caused discouragement and led to the demise of the church. Chapman, however, was convinced that he had taken the right course. Because the remaining church was solidly behind him, he continued on.

At about the time Chapman came to Barnstaple, a General Baptist (distinct from Particular Baptist) church was constituted there. A new building was erected for them by the owner of the lace factory and was completed in February of 1833, ten months after Chapman arrived. But the General Baptist work did not thrive and collapsed in about three years. The property was put up for sale, but a sale never materialized. The seceders from Ebenezer asked to rent the building and were permitted to do so, although meeting as Particular Baptists. After another year or so the General Baptists regrouped and asked the Particular Baptists to vacate the building. At that point the seceders from Ebenezer demanded that Chapman's group abandon Ebenezer Chapel on the ground that they were not using it in accordance with the original intention and practices of Particular Baptists.

Chapman carefully inspected the trust deed to Ebenezer Chapel and found that no provisions had been violated. But the seceders persisted and Chapman became convinced that the Scriptural position was simply to give them the building. He didn't want anyone to think that he had secured the building through cunning. The situation was equivalent, he said, to giving up one's coat to someone who demanded it, which was Christ's admonition. The congregation agreed and handed the title to the building over to the seceders about 1838.

Such a unified action by these Christians seems almost unbelievable. They gave up their building—their legal claim—to a group of dissidents. How many Christian leaders, how many churches, would have done such a thing? Shouldn't they have stood up for their rights? By this unusual action these Christians illustrated the principle of Christlike love and the reward was great. A generation later the Barnstaple Baptists comprised a strong evangelistic group. Their writings reveal a great respect and admiration for Robert Chapman, whom many think of as one of their pioneers. Baptist records show, however, that Chapman's group was not associated with the Baptists from about the time of the secession.

THE SEARCH FOR ANOTHER MEETING PLACE

In the late 1830s the tanyard at the end of New Buildings Street—the street where Chapman lived—closed down and the property was put up for sale. Chapman's group, which now referred to itself simply as an "Assembly of Christians" in order to avoid any denominational connotation, decided to buy this desirable piece of land. It was several blocks from the original chapel and just a few steps from Chapman's house. The other side of the parcel opened onto Bear Street—the main street leading east out of town. The lot was much larger than the Assembly needed at that time, but the congregation had been growing steadily and this property would permit future expansion.

After Chapman completed the legal documents for the transfer of the property, the local clergy of the Anglican church made it known that they had intended to buy that ground for a new parish church. The surprised Assembly met to decide what to do and prayed for guidance. Chapman was led to Philippians 4:5, which says, "Let your forbearing spirit be known to all men. The Lord is near" (NASB). He advised the Assembly to give up its claim. Once again it did, apparently without any squabbling. The remarkable spirit demonstrated by Chapman and the entire church is another good example of how the Christian life can illustrate Scripture. And once again the outcome was favorable. When the Anglicans erected their building a few years later, their church had an evangelical orientation, and in this Chapman and his group probably had much influence.

A NEW CHURCH HOME

The Christians who relinquished Ebenezer Chapel were no longer a small group. They were vigorous, evangelistic, and well known in Barnstaple, but for a while they had no building of their own in which to meet. From about 1838 to 1842 they probably met in rented quarters on Sundays. They used Chapman's home at No. 6 New Buildings Street for midweek meetings. By 1839 they were using Elizabeth Paget's home at No. 9 New Buildings Street for the Thursday evening Bible studies. But in spite of adversity they continued to grow.

The Assembly had recovered its deposit after the abortive attempt to purchase the ground of the former tanyard and had money enough to purchase a modest property. About 1840 several small streets were laid out on either side of Bear Street adjacent to the Derby area. Building plots on those streets became available for purchase. The Assembly saw this area as an answer to its needs: just a few blocks from Ebenezer, close to the poor people, and a five-to-ten-minute walk from the town center. One of the new lanes, Grosvenor Street, extended north from Bear Street. There the Assembly purchased a lot and erected a large plain structure. They finished construction and occupied Bear Street Chapel in 1842, ten years after Chapman arrived in Barnstaple. Much larger than Ebenezer Chapel, it could seat 450 people.

Many dissenting churches as well as individuals of that day considered it a matter of faith not to incur any debt. However we know that the Barnstaple Assembly had taken on a debt in order to finish construction, for Müller states in his *Narrative of the Lord's Dealings with George Müller* that in 1843 he forwarded to Barnstaple a sum of money which had been designated for "the completion of payment of expenses" incurred in building the chapel there. Thus the debt was short-lived and the work from that time was free of financial encumbrance.

CONFIDENT IN THE LORD

The first years in Barnstaple were very challenging for Chapman. The joys of ministry success had been mixed with strife and potential discouragement. Thomas Pugsley—Chapman's friend, relative, and staunch supporter—died in 1834, as did Chapman's younger brother Thomas. Ebenezer Chapel had grown rapidly but had experienced division. Key properties had been surrendered. Two young men who had developed into good preachers, leaders, and evangelists had left for India. But Chapman remained strong and confident in the Lord.

A look down Bear Street around 1870.

Left, Grosvenor Street Chapel in 1988, known as Bear Street Chapel in its early days.
(photo courtesy of the author)

Right, the inside of Grosvenor Street Chapel in 1988 before it was sold.
(photo courtesy of the author)

Harington Evans remained Chapman's constant supporter. In 1842 Evans wrote a letter from his residence in London: "R. Chapman has just left us. He slept here last night, after preaching for me at John Street. Oh, what a man of God is he! What grace does he exhibit! Courage, meekness, love, self-denial, tenderness, perseverance, love for souls—all springing out of love of Christ and God—seem beauteously blended together in beautiful symmetry."

Evans' respect and love for Chapman continued to grow. In 1846 he again visited Barnstaple and wrote, "I found beloved R. Chapman all that he ever was, and more—more like Christ, more self-denying, gentle, and full of love." Later that year Evans told a friend, "He is one of my stars. I hold him to be one of the first men of the age. He has no ebbs or flows. He can always realize his acceptance. But then he is indeed a child, ready for anything, everything—it matters not what." Once he discipled Chapman; now he saw a true leader and servant.

"He has no ebbs or flows," Evans had written. Chapman knew that the absence of the seceders would allow a more unified development of the work. Knowing that God had called Bowden and Beer, Chapman was happy to see them advance. Robert Gribble had returned to the area and was active again. Thomas Pugsley was now rejoicing with the Lord, and Charles Shepherd—a local person—had taken up much of the work in the chapels where Pugsley had been working. Shepherd, who became acquainted with Harington Evans during Evans' frequent visits to North Devon, later accepted the pastorate of John Street Chapel in London when Evans died.

Thus God's work continued. God is sovereign and Chapman never questioned the seemingly difficult events that unfolded.

8
A Burden for Spain

When Robert Chapman began to sense God's call to fulltime Christian work a few years after his conversion, his thoughts turned first to missions. Italy had long been on his heart, and Spain occupied his thoughts as well. His burden for Spain, Portugal, and Italy was a result of the stranglehold that a corrupted Roman Catholicism had on the people of those countries, which practically prevented them from knowing the true God. Superstition prevailed. Some priests showed great cynicism toward all things religious and many of them discouraged people from reading the Bible. But Chapman knew that the Bible was written for the common man. It was given for guidance, instruction, and reproof and it was not the sole possession of any elite group.

Chapman wanted to find a way to bring the good news of Christ to the common people of Spain. That country, with its glorious and inglorious religious history, was known for its persecution of evangelicals and was closed to foreign missionaries. Believing that he might someday have a missionary work in the Iberian peninsula, Chapman studied Spanish and Portuguese until he could speak both fluently. And when the Lord set Chapman's course for Barnstaple, his interest in Spain and missionary work did not diminish. A great portion of his activity in North Devon was tantamount to missionary work, but he still wondered if he could somehow merge that work with missionary activity in Spain. He knew he had a gift for interacting with people and, since Spain was so much on his mind, was convinced that God would have him go.

THE FIRST EXPLORATORY TRIP

After just two years in Barnstaple, Chapman took a short trip to Spain. Little is known of it. Chapman probably went as a tourist so that he could assess firsthand what he or others might encounter there on a subsequent mission. England was at that time an ally of Spain, having recently helped to drive the French out of the country. In 1833 Isabella II was proclaimed queen of Spain, but her government was vigorously and sometimes violently opposed by the Carlists who favored her uncle, Don Carlos. For many years the Carlists used terrorist tactics in attempts to bring down the government and at times anarchy nearly ruled. Thus travel through Spain was by no means safe. But far from being disheartened by what he learned, Chapman resolved to make an extended missionary trip to Spain as soon as possible.

After his return to Barnstaple, Chapman emphasized the spiritual need of Spain and Portugal in his sermons and urged listeners to consider devoting their lives to the service of God in those countries. These repeated words had effect; two men in the Assembly, Messrs. Pick and Handcock, expressed a strong interest in going there.

THE FIRST MISSIONARY TRIP

In 1838 Chapman made plans to return to Spain. Pick and Handcock would go with him. This was the time during which the flock Chapman was shepherding lacked its own building, but he felt confident enough in the leadership present in the congregation to leave for a few months. Knowing that any public preaching in Spain would be severely limited and perhaps impossible, he planned to walk throughout the country, talking to individuals about Christ and giving them Bibles. He would carry just his backpack containing some clothes and smuggled Bibles.

There is an interesting dilemma here. Chapman decided to break the law of the land and he seemed to have had no misgivings about it. When man's law violates God's law, he believed that God's law must prevail. Chapman was also quite aware of the response of Peter and the other apostles in a similar situation recorded in Acts 5:27-29.

Many friends urged him not to go since Spain had passed laws making it illegal to preach outside the Roman Catholic system. But Chapman remained determined to go. Seeing that they could not dissuade him and knowing that he knew no one in Spain and had only his backpack and enough money for the fares, some friends collected a sum of money and presented him with a check just before he left. The three missionaries traveled first to London, where Chapman visited with many friends at John Street Chapel. From there they traveled to the port of Gravesend, just east of London on the Thames river, and boarded a ship that would take them to France.

The unanticipated check caused Chapman great concern. His plan had been to rely in faith on God's provision for his necessities as his trip progressed. The possibility that God might provide for his necessities before the trip started apparently was not a part of Chapman's thinking. When the ship was on the North Sea, Chapman, in the presence of his companions, took out the check and tore it up. "Now I shall be entirely dependent upon God," he said.

How his friends back home reacted to this piece of news is not known. It certainly could have been insulting to them. Surely Chapman knew that God usually provides for His work through His people. Why he could not bring himself to accept the check is a puzzle. Perhaps he had made a vow not to have any money with him as he traveled through Spain. Or his refusal may have been an evidence of spiritual pride, for many years later he said that spiritual pride had been his biggest problem as a young Christian.

Traveling south through France, the three men passed through Bayonne, taking the coastal route along the bay of Biscay and entering Spain near the town of San Sebastian. This was Basque country and the Basques found it in their own interests to support the Carlists against the government. A garrison of English soldiers was stationed at San Sebastian, perhaps to provide stability. Chapman and his companions secured permission to talk to the soldiers, who were only too happy to receive fellow Englishmen. Before leaving, Chapman managed to preach a sermon to them.

Pick and Handcock accompanied him to about this point, but then Chapman seems to have traveled alone. He walked through the breadth and length of the country, carrying his backpack holding the forbidden Scriptures. He rarely found a believer, but he frequently witnessed to people while on the roads. Chapman later told of his encounter with a priest during this trip:

> While I was travelling in Spain, some time before any railways had been constructed, I placed my bag, etc., in a kind of caravan, and shortly after was joined by a Roman Catholic priest. There was no third person present. About this time the question as to whether Mary, the mother of our Lord, was a sinner or not was being mooted amongst the Romanists. The Pope brought the matter to a head by asserting she was not a sinner, so the matter came up in our conversation; so I said to my friend the priest, "Now hear what the Word of God says:

'Mary saith, my soul doth magnify the Lord, and my spirit doth rejoice in God my Savior.'" Whereupon I added, "How could she rejoice in God her Savior if she had never sinned?" So the priest replied gravely, "Quite true, quite true." He would not have said that had there been a third person present.

The journey was indeed perilous. "While I was walking along in a very lonely place in a certain part of Spain," Chapman said later, "two men came up behind me, and I heard them say, 'He is alone; let us rob him.' I immediately lifted up my heart to God and sought deliverance; the answer came back at once, and the men left me without further annoyance."

Chapman worked his way westward across Spain to the Atlantic coast. Seeing the tall mountain El Castilo, he climbed to its summit and surveyed the country that at the beginning of the Christian era had known such blessing. His journey near its end, Chapman knelt on the summit and prayed that God would intervene in Spain and allow the light of the gospel to penetrate its spiritual darkness. Confident of God's answer to his prayer, he wrote back to Barnstaple, "We shall establish our evangelists here." Two dozen years later he saw his prayers and hopes come to fruition. The doors to Spain opened and Protestant missionaries were allowed to enter.

We know little else about Chapman's 1838 trip, but it accomplished its purpose. Many hearts were stirred in England because of the stories he told of his experiences, and widespread missionary interest in Spain developed. Quite a few men and women decided to carry the gospel to Spain and Chapman ministered to them in many ways. He worked alongside them when he was there, preaching and distributing literature. A constant stream of encouraging letters flowed from his pen when he was home. His prayers for the missionaries were unceasing and they knew it. When they came back to England on furlough, he insisted that they rest at his home when they could. Although his life's work was centered in Barnstaple,

Chapman was a pioneer missionary to Spain and a source of strength to others.

Henry Payne of Barnstaple, one of those influenced by Chapman to go to Spain as a missionary, heard Chapman speak of his 1838 visit and the spiritual condition in Spain. Payne wrote:

> When Mr. Chapman determined to visit Spain... nothing moved him from his purpose. He told his friends that he counted on God for help in all circumstances, that he was persuaded it was the will of the Lord that he should go; and...if an assassin took his life...it would...give him entrance to his Father's home above. He travelled through the country, generally on foot, in order to have better opportunities for speaking to persons alone. He found the people, as a rule, ready to listen to him when no one was near to overhear what was being said. Even then the people hated the clergy, but fear caused them to be exceedingly reserved. No doubt Mr. Chapman's countenance, which revealed his kindness of heart, was a great help to him in securing the ear of the people. He told me that one day when he was seated in a [public stagecoach] in Spain, though he had not opened his lips, a man and a woman began to quarrel furiously in French, and at last the woman said, "I affirm that I am as innocent of that of which you accuse me as is that holy man of God sitting in the corner, who anyone can see is going straight to heaven."

During the 1840s and 1850s several Christian organizations worked to get the gospel into Spain. The British and Foreign Bible Society, with which Chapman had established an affiliation, gradually began making inroads, distributing Bibles and literature. But the government still aggressively suppressed Protestant evangelism by native Spaniards. During these years the Lord raised up a young Spanish evangelist, Manuel Matamoros, who received worldwide attention after being imprisoned for his success in bringing many to Christ. His sentence, nine years in the galleys, was commuted, but he was banished to the town of Bayonne, just over the border into France. Chapman corresponded with the exiled Matamoros, offering encouragement, and on his next trip to Spain he visited and counseled him.

9

Bear Street Chapel: A Church Alive

The Barnstaple Assembly often referred to its new building just north of Bear Street as simply "The Room." It was well named, for at the beginning it was essentially just one large room—a large square box. The ceiling was very high and the windows were placed high up on the walls. This was probably done because adjacent buildings, built very close by, would have blocked the light had the windows been lower. The furnishings were plain, even rough, and were probably made by members of the congregation, including Chapman. The pews were benches. The Assembly made no provision for a baptistery, although Ebenezer Chapel had one; all baptizing took place in the Taw river. At the front of the room a small platform was built, about three steps high. On this stood a podium from which the preacher delivered his sermon. A wall behind the platform defined the end of the meeting room and provided a space on the other side where mothers with small children usually stayed during the preaching services.

England conducted an ecclesiastical census in 1851, in which information on all the establishment and nonconformist churches in the country was collected. The records show some interesting information about the Barnstaple Assembly. One census form was filled out for the Assembly by Samuel Ware, one of the members, for March of that year. Chapman completed another such form at the end of the year. The two forms show that an average of three hundred people attended the preaching service on Sunday mornings, not including the Sunday school students who numbered about one hundred. About one hundred fifty people attended the Sunday evening meeting. Both Chapman and Ware recorded that their building was erected in 1842, a useful fact since other memorials written about Chapman placed the date several years later. Under the heading *Denomination* Ware put simply "Christians" and Chapman entered "Christian Brethren." Ware called the chapel "Bear Street Meeting House" and Chapman called it "Bear Street Chapel." These differences show that the Christians there had given neither themselves nor their building any special name, in keeping with Chapman's attitudes. Many years later the building was named "Grosvenor Street Chapel." In his correspondence Chapman addressed the Assembly as the "Christians Assembled at Bear Street."

CHURCH LEADERSHIP STYLE DEFINED

From existing materials and correspondence it is difficult to tell just when Chapman and other leaders at the Barnstaple Assembly instituted a recognized plural leadership. This style of leadership probably crystallized soon after 1839 when George Müller and Henry Craik instituted a recognized eldership at Bethesda Chapel in Bristol. The term *elders* was being used at the Bear Street Chapel by the 1850s. Still the people considered Chapman to be the "first among equals." This was not because he insisted that it be so. Rather his leadership qualities of humility, gentleness, and loving concern made him so. Like the apostle

Peter among the twelve disciples, he was the prominent elder.

Chapman did the majority of the preaching for the Assembly until his last decade of life. His own technique for preparing a sermon was to make copious notes during his daily meditations. These would fix in his mind what he would say, but he seems not to have used any notes when preaching. He insisted that any teacher or preacher be first of all a student of the Bible; he must be constantly immersed in it and keep it at the center of his life. No one was allowed to develop ideas in isolation from the Assembly, although much latitude was allowed. When someone preached in a way that was not particularly helpful, Chapman or another elder would speak to the person.

Formal training in preaching or speaking was rare among the smaller dissenting churches, and Bear Street Chapel was no exception. The speakers learned "on the job." Just as Chapman had developed his preaching skills largely at London's John Street Chapel under the tutelage of Harington Evans, young men at Bear Street Chapel were encouraged by Chapman and other elders to develop their skills. The open Lord's Supper of the Assembly, during which any man could rise to speak briefly, was also a natural starting point in learning to address an audience.

Henry Heath was one of those who became a preacher as well as a leader at the Bear Street Chapel. He was studying for holy orders in the Anglican church when in 1839 he secured a position as schoolmaster at the school run by the Anglicans at Tawstock, which was very close to the chapel where Thomas Pugsley had ministered. Soon after arriving, Heath heard about Robert Chapman and secured an introduction, likely through the Wrey family, whose daughter Chapman had baptized a few years earlier. Chapman invited Heath to the Thursday evening Bible readings he was then holding at No. 9 New Buildings Street. Seeing no conflict in this with his studies within the Anglican church, Heath accepted and became a regular attendee. He was impressed by the simple manner Chapman used in expounding the Scriptures. The Holy

Spirit began working in him and he soon became exercised about his purpose in life.

The Scriptures became a new power to Heath's soul and not just a theological work suited for his mind. His frequent visits to Chapman's simple dwelling and his observation of Chapman's manner of life and trust in the Scriptures made Heath want to follow that path. After much prayer, waiting on God for direction, and no doubt receiving much counsel from Chapman, Heath gave up his studies for holy orders in the Anglican church. He kept his position as schoolmaster at the Anglican school, but joined Chapman in the work with the Barnstaple Assembly about the time the Assembly moved into Bear Street Chapel. He became a leader there and Chapman recognized that he was a dedicated man of God. Many people said later that he much resembled Chapman in his demeanor.

In 1846 Chapman commended Heath in a letter: "Through his grace and gift he has so commended himself to all, that he is received as a peculiar boon of a Father's love." Heath moved in 1848 to Hackney, a town on the north side of London, where he preached and worked in another Assembly for twenty-one years. Although he achieved a reputation as an excellent preacher and was much in demand among the Brethren, he did not desire fame. In 1869 he moved to the tiny isolated village of Woolpit, about seventy-five miles northeast of London. There he ministered to people of all ranks for the remainder of his life. Chapman stayed in close contact with Heath and said, "There was always Henry Heath's room at our house ready for him when he came."

In addition to the emphasis on Biblical preaching and weekly observance of the Lord's Supper, the Christians at Bear Street Chapel also loved to sing. They had no piano and the hymnal they used provided no musical accompaniment—not uncommon at that time. Chapman and others among the Brethren wrote many of the hymns sung at Bear Street Chapel. Most of these composers simply wrote the words and fit them to existing tunes, so a melody often had to serve many different hymns. The Assembly decided to have midweek singing practice for those who loved to sing and could take the lead on Sundays. The practice was usually held at Chapman's home.

ACTIVE SUNDAY SCHOOL MINISTRY

A Sunday school work for the children of the neighborhood was another concern of the Assembly, but fulfillment of this need seems to have waited until Elizabeth Paget arrived in the late 1830s. In most churches of that time it was accepted that women should not take leadership roles in church meetings. This was the pattern in New Testament times and Chapman wanted the Assembly to be consistent with the practice. Bessie Paget was one of the faithful, but she was not content merely to be a listener. Back in the 1820s she had started a church in the village of Poltimore; now she accepted male leadership at the Assembly, placed herself into the system, and found ways to use her gifts. Opening her home as she did was one of these ways; initiating the afternoon Sunday school was another.

At first the Sunday school was held in a rented hall on Union Street, close to New Buildings Street. Apparently it was begun before the construction of Bear Street Chapel. The children of the poor in the Derby area were brought in, taught stories from the Bible, and—under Miss Paget's firm but loving eyes—shown a measure of discipline that many of them did not receive in their own homes.

A DAY SCHOOL BEGINS

Before free state education came to England and other countries, many churches ran their own schools. The Bear Street Assembly decided to do this also and added two or three school rooms to the chapel in 1856. All the teachers were members of the Assembly and the successive headmasters were recognized elders there. The chapel was enlarged as the Assembly grew, including the construction of a large balcony. One account written about 1870 asserted that Chapman regularly preached to seven hundred people each Sunday.

By about 1880 the Christians at Bear Street Chapel were planning to build a larger day school in which Chapman and two other elders would provide the religious instruction. One of the earls of the realm, Lord Fortescue, lived in North Devon not far from Barnstaple and knew of Chapman, whom he greatly respected. When Lord Fortescue learned that the Assembly desired to build a day school, he willingly supported the project with his funds. The Assembly in 1883 purchased a tiny graveyard east of the chapel, and the building was enlarged to accommodate the school. Curiously some of the gravestones were incorporated into the floor. For many years Lord Fortescue insisted that the annual Sunday school and day school outings be held at his estate.

OUTREACH TO THE POOR

The Bear Street Chapel also felt an obligation to assist the poor in their area. Bessie set up a soup kitchen in her house with the assistance of many in the Assembly. The congregation also collected clothing and distributed it to the poor. One of Chapman's good deeds illustrates the depth of love and compassion the members of the Assembly showed to the poverty-stricken. Once given a new coat by a friend, he soon gave it to a poor man living nearby. After a while the friend remarked on the absence of the coat and Chapman confessed that he had given it away. He always preached that such behavior should not be considered extraordinary for a Christian. He frequently quoted from Luke 3:11, "He that hath two coats, let him impart to him that hath none."

Thus the Assembly at Bear Street Chapel began a long tradition of social work. The Assembly was a complete church. Demonstrating a New Testament spirit of love and vitality, it had good preaching from the Bible, a separate time for worship and remembrance, active involvement by members who loved each other, a large Sunday school, evangelistic concern for the people of the community, and a concern for the material needs of the poor. It was a church alive.

10
Chapman's Hospitality House

C hapman frequently told people that he had many trials of faith but that trials are sent to strengthen faith. His retreat for the Lord's servants was one arena in which his faith was tested. Often his guests or their friends sent money or provisions to Chapman. Sometimes, however, provisions ran low and there was no money to buy supplies. Anxious when he first started his hospitality ministry, Chapman came to understand that God was arranging things for each day. When the funds ran out, he would pray about it and soon there would be money for food. Childlike dependence on God became a habit and he tried to convey to his friends that this was the natural attitude of a child of God.

Another trial of faith soon awaited him. Although several Christian workers came at the outset of his hospitality ministry, not long afterward his visitors began dwindling in numbers. This perplexed him, for he had been convinced of God's leading in this work. He examined his motives. Was a false humility at work here? Was pride deceiving him? He took the problem to God. In prayer he cried, "Why, Lord, dost Thou not send Thy children to me?" Perhaps the Lord was waiting for Chapman's humbling, for soon after that visitors began coming again. From that time on there was a steady flow.

After Bessie Paget came to Barnstaple, the rest home was expanded to include her home across the narrow street. The meals were taken there, and Chapman also had a sitting room there in which he did his writing and received visitors. After each meal Chapman led his guests in a hymn, gave a brief word from the Scriptures, and offered a prayer for all. Conversation at the meals was not allowed to become frivolous and Chapman quickly turned any complaining or gossipy talk toward more fruitful ground.

One of Chapman's customs was to clean the shoes or boots of his visitors. After showing arriving guests to their rooms, he would instruct them to leave their footwear outside their doors so that he could clean them by the next morning. Typically they objected to his doing such a menial task, but he was quite insistent. One guest recorded Chapman's answer to his objections: "It is not the custom in our day to wash one another's feet; that which most nearly corresponds to this command of the Lord is to clean each other's boots."

A worker in Hudson Taylor's ministry in China, J. Norman Case, related how he first heard about Chapman's "sound and helpful ministry" at a Bible conference, probably about 1875. After that he spent two months at Chapman's house, under the tutelage of Chapman and William Hake, who was then living in Barnstaple. Case wrote:

> The whole ordering of the household had in view not only the comfort, but the general spiritual, mental, and physical well-being of the many who came there for rest. It struck me at the time as being in its arrangement and conduct an ideal Christian household. The wisdom of retiring and rising early was forcibly taught by precept and example. Love and

reverence for the Scriptures, and subjection thereto, formed the very atmosphere of the house. There, too, the "table-talk" was turned to spiritual ends as I have never to the same degree elsewhere known. An ordinary meal became an agape, more helpful than many a long meeting. The living was plain but good. It was recognized fully that the body was the Lord's, and should be treated accordingly. It was an ideal home for a tired or discouraged worker, or for a despondent or perplexed Christian. There one seemed naturally to be in that state of mind to hear the question and heed the exhortation to one of old: "Seekest thou great things for thyself? Seek them not." A stay there of days or weeks could not but deeply influence the whole aftercourse of a young Christian.

A clergyman of the Church of England, H. B. Macartney, heard of Chapman and his rest home and decided to visit the remarkable man. He arranged to stay several days in 1878, when Chapman was seventy-five years old, and afterward chronicled his impressions in a book. Macartney wrote:

We all retired to rest about nine o'clock last night; for the hours at New Buildings are particularly early—breakfast at seven, dinner at noon. Mr. Chapman always retires at nine and rises at four. From four o'clock until twelve he is principally occupied with God. It was laid on his heart very soon after his affections had become fixed on better things, that the world stood in great need of intercession, and that intercession was to be peculiarly his vocation; therefore his first and best hours are given to prayer. Devotion does not, however, in any way interfere with the energies of life. He preaches to 800 souls every Sunday; he undertakes pastoral work; he attends to the minutest bodily and spiritual wants of a stream of visitors, some of whom stay for an hour, some for a month; he is the mainspring of a great evangelistic and Bible work in England and

Spain; he corresponds with men like George Müller, and with seekers and workers in various parts of the world. Nor is he shut up during those first eight hours. For instance, it was his practice, till quite recently, to go round to every door and take away the boots of his guests, to clean them with his own hands. He called me at my own request at five. I was awake and waiting for his step. He put his venerable head in at my door just at the hour, lighting my candle and giving me for my morning portion: "As for God, His way is perfect." A little after, he came to guide me to a little sitting-room, where a chair and warm rug were placed beside a table furnished with a reading lamp, and just in front of a lovely fire. At six o'clock I heard him calling one of the married couples in an adjacent room, with the words, "I will fear no evil."...We breakfasted by lamplight at seven o'clock, and Mr. Chapman, who had prepared his own breakfast earlier, joined us at eight o'clock for family worship.

After dinner at twelve o'clock I explored the neighborhood a little, till it was time for the Bible reading at half-past three. The Song of Solomon occupied our thoughts till nearly six o'clock, when we had tea, during which fresh visitors from a distance came in intending to stay for the night. But at seven o'clock, Mr. Chapman, according to promise, took me away with Mr. Hake to a little room at the end of the courtyard, which I had not seen before, and for two hours unfolded to me his thoughts and researches on prophecy; and with the gentlest, and with what it almost seems presumption to call the most teachable spirit, sought to know my mind. This is what strikes me most of all in the retrospect; that a man so well born, so well educated, muscularly so strong and vigorous, such a traveller, so much sought after, one who knows the Lord face to face, should be so lowly. But the last characteristic accounts for it all—communion with God makes him childlike.

Macartney also described the last day of his visit:

> Prayer and breakfast ended, I visited Mr.
> Chapman's workshop; carried away a bread platter
> cut by his own lathe, took farewell of good old Mr.
> Hake and some of the other guests....We walked to-
> gether by a lonely road to the station. This was the
> most profitable time I have yet had. I asked him
> many questions about the Christian life, and got the
> broadest, most comprehensive answers. I told him
> of a dear friend of mine, a perfectionist, who said he
> had got back to Adam's state—no sin in him, but
> only the possibility of sinning if he did not watch.
> "Adam's state!" he said with vehemence. "Back to
> Adam's state! I would not change places with Adam
> before the fall, for a hundred thousand worlds!"
> Speaking of prayer, he said, "When I bow to God,
> God stoops to me." Speaking of wholehearted ser-
> vice, he said, "As the father and child do all that they
> can to please each other, so I do all I can to please
> God, and God does all He can to please me." On the
> subject of gaining the mastery over besetting sins,
> he was very positive. He said, "Give yourself to at-
> tacking the filthiness of the spirit more than the
> filthiness of the flesh—pride, selfishness, self-seek-
> ing, etc.—these are the ring-leaders; aim at them.
> Fight ye not with small or great, save only with the
> King of Israel. While you are occupied in gaining the
> victory over little sins, great sins will be occupied in
> gaining the victory over you. When great sins are
> overcome, little sins fall with them." Thus we
> reached the train—in falling snow and bitter cold,
> but our hearts were full.

The rest home was from time to time made available
to people other than the Lord's workers and it appears
that some guests paid Chapman a fee. On one occasion a
couple from the United States were vacationing in
Barnstaple and staying at one of its best hotels. They

heard about Chapman and paid him a visit. During the conversation the lady remarked on how noisy the hotel was, whereupon Chapman invited them to stay with him and they promptly had their belongings moved to his house. A letter written in the mid-1840s includes the comment that the writer and her cousin decided not to stay overnight at Chapman's, citing the cost of the room as one of the reasons!

The Chapman rest home became very popular during the seventy years that Chapman lived at No. 6 New Buildings. It expanded to No. 9 when Bessie Paget arrived in Barnstaple and after the Hakes moved there. At a later point, increasing numbers of guests necessitated the purchase and use of No. 8, next door to Chapman. Chapman's vision for a place of rest and encouragement was richly fulfilled.

11
Personal Habits

Robert Chapman enjoyed rising very early each morning to go for a long walk until advanced age made it impossible. He was very health-conscious and walked for his body's sake, not merely for pleasure. With his long legs and rapid gait he covered great distances in brief times. Occasionally he walked to Ilfracombe, twelve miles north of Barnstaple on the coast of the Bristol channel, for breakfast. When he had guests, however, he usually walked a few miles and then returned in time to clean their boots and shoes and call them for breakfast. His walking habit became well known, and perhaps some mythology developed concerning it. Someone once claimed that Chapman walked to Exeter, arriving in time for the mid-day meal! (It must have been a late meal because Exeter was about forty miles away.) Another person said that Chapman walked twenty-five miles before breakfast, which could have been possible had he started at 3:00 a.m. for a breakfast served at 9:00 a.m.

But more likely, admiration for Chapman created occasional exaggeration.

We have seen that Chapman did not confine his ministry to Ebenezer Chapel during his first years in Barnstaple, but visited and evangelized throughout the town and neighboring villages. These habits did not change after Bear Street Chapel was built in 1842. For more than fifty years he walked throughout the countryside to these villages and preached in their chapels. Many Brethren assemblies started up throughout North Devon after he arrived and although they had their own leaders, Chapman took special interest in their well-being.

One of his walks took an interesting twist, although Chapman probably never knew of it. He said on many occasions that in spite of the fact that he had never seen an angel, he certainly believed in their existence because the Bible spoke of them. One of H. W. Soltau's sons related the following story told to him by a villager: The villager's brother had become so angry at Chapman's preaching in a village near Barnstaple that he swore he would kill him. One day he returned to his house clearly shaken. When his brother asked what had happened, he said that he had been waiting along a quiet road with his gun, knowing that Chapman would pass that way alone on his way back to Barnstaple. But, he said, he could not shoot him because another man was always between him and Chapman.

Chapman liked to pray—to commune with God—while engaged in physical activities. Life for the Christian should be filled with prayer and for him it was. He also established a regular schedule of Bible study on weekdays, setting aside the mornings for Bible reading and for meditation on what he had read. His constant reading of God's Word made it so familiar to him that he was able to apply it readily to situations that occur in everyone's life. For this reason he was valued as a counselor and was frequently asked to intervene and give advice in family situations even though he never married.

Chapman, who was frugal and did not permit food to be wasted, composed the following poem for the children of a friend:

If mustard or salt I take more than I use,
Let straightway my conscience the waster accuse;
My Lord who redeemed me, whose Name is my boast,
Said "Gather the fragments, that nothing be lost."

A friend remembered that Chapman more than once commented on not wasting food while he was a dinner guest at another's house. Ordinarily this would not endear a person to his or her host, but he was so gracious that it was not taken as an offense. Because of the way he lived, people realized that he was not fussy, but desired to put principles into action.

Habits from Chapman's upper-class childhood may be seen in the fact that he installed a lead-lined bathtub in his bedroom. He took a hot bath at night just before going to bed and a cold bath in the morning. A product of his time concerning matters of health, he explained that it was important to open the pores of the body at night and close them in the morning. He ate carefully and according to the accepted standards of the day. Chapman's housekeeper stated that when he was older, he fixed himself two eggs for breakfast and drank a cup of cocoa or milk the last thing before retiring. If his diet seems not to be the best according to our present standards, we need to remember that Chapman usually was in excellent health and that he lived to age ninety-nine. Chapman often remarked that the body is to be used for God's service and therefore people must take good care of their bodies.

He was equally aware of the need for proper care of the mind, as shown by his desire to provide a place of rest for Christian workers. Some of these workers drove themselves relentlessly. Often their continuous activities took the place of personal time with the Lord, so their minds never received needed breaks from the daily routines. Aware of this danger, Chapman provided for his own relaxation, which took place each Saturday. He fitted out a woodworking shop in a tiny room at the rear of his house. It contained a set of quality tools and a lathe. He spent most of each Saturday in this shop and discouraged his friends from visiting him there. This was also a day of fasting for him. Through the years he produced many fine pieces of furniture, including a desk and some items that were used in Bear Street Chapel. He gave bowls and breadboards to some of his guests and he sold some pieces to set up a fund for missionary support.

Chapman believed that he shouldn't vote in public elections, a common attitude among many Christians at that time. According to his housekeeper, however, town councilors and members of Parliament visited him at his home. "When putting up for election [they] would have a good talk with him. He would always say, 'Dear Brother, I can't vote for you but I can pray for you.'" This account and his friendship with Lord Fortescue show the great respect Chapman had gained among the area's leaders even though he would not engage in politics. Obviously the politicians believed that he could influence many votes.

12
A Long Walk around Ireland

Robert Chapman's missionary trip through Spain in 1838 had shown him that the spiritual state of that country was low and open evangelism was dangerous, so his thoughts turned toward Ireland. The nonconformist movement in Ireland had never attained the influence or zeal that it had in England. The eighteenth-century revivals under Whitefield and Wesley that transformed much of the life of England had made fewer inroads into Ireland. The influence of the Church of Ireland—the Irish arm of the Church of England—had seriously eroded, and the Roman Catholic Church was rapidly gaining strength. Chapman, although broad-minded in his view of Christian unity, was disturbed over the effects of Roman Catholicism. He was concerned that it would do in Ireland what it had done in Spain. There Catholicism was not only steeped in superstition; some priests openly derided religion, turning people away from God. After the mid-1840s, Chapman had other reasons to visit Ireland.

A divergence of views on Christian unity had developed among the Assemblies. By then J. N. Darby, who believed the church age was at an end, was promoting the view that Christians should separate themselves from all existing churches and their organizations. He also argued that the Assemblies should be strongly interconnected. These were not Chapman's views, nor those of Groves, Müller, Craik, or many other leaders in the new movement, but Darby—a constant traveler among the Assemblies and a prolific pamphleteer—was quite successful in spreading his beliefs. At the end of 1845 a troubling event occurred. Darby, following a conflict with B. W. Newton, set up a rival Assembly in Plymouth, a move that brought the question of unity into sharp focus. Chapman attempted to mediate with Darby, but to no avail. The strife and confusion in Plymouth increased and at the end of 1847 Newton left the city under a cloud. Of all the prominent figures among the Brethren, Darby was the best known and most influential in Ireland. So Chapman wanted to visit with the leading Brethren in Ireland to assess their views and to share his views in turn.

Yet another reason to visit Ireland pressed upon Chapman's mind. A severe famine was underway, a result of the failure of the potato crops through disease. About 750,000 people died of starvation or disease from 1845 to 1847. The tales of misery and death were almost unbelievable. With Chapman's encouragement, Bear Street Chapel had started sending money to support the efforts of an Anglican rector and his wife who had established an orphanage near Cork for children whose parents had died in the famine. The Christians at Bear Street Chapel did not let differences with the Church of England stop them from supporting a vital effort.

Chapman decided that the time was right for an extended visit to Ireland—that once-beautiful but now devastated land. As 1847 drew to a close, he laid out an itinerary and purposed to visit and encourage the poor and those who were helping the poor. He would counsel and encourage the many Assemblies that had sprung up in Ireland and consult with their leaders. In order to reach as many Roman Catholics as possible, he decided to preach in open-air meetings if that was permitted. No aloof preacher, Chapman determined to travel mostly on foot, as he had in Spain, in order to engage people while he walked from town to town.

A. N. Groves had written from India that he planned to return to England for rest and ministry in the spring of 1848. Perhaps Chapman arranged his trip to begin in February so that he could be back in time to see Groves. Winters in Ireland are generally not severe, so travel would not be especially difficult, although not particularly pleasant for one traveling on foot. In contrast to his 1838 visit to Spain, when he hadn't known a single Christian or any other person there before setting out, Chapman was able to set up a rough timetable of contact points throughout Ireland.

Leaving the Christians at Bear Street Chapel in the care of Henry Heath and others, Chapman left Barnstaple by coach for the day's journey east to the port city of Bristol. Presumably he could have taken a boat to Ireland from Barnstaple or Bideford, but he wanted first to visit his many friends and seek their prayers. On the evening before his departure a small group met; George Müller offered a prayer for his well-being and a fruitful journey. On February 1, 1848, Chapman boarded a boat bound for the city of Cork on the southern coast of Ireland. His journey, which would last three months, would demand a great deal of stamina, but the forty-five-year-old Chapman was in the prime of life and very strong.

He agreed to keep a journal and send weekly letters back to Barnstaple, to be read by Henry Heath "to the Children of God, assembling in Bear Street." One of his letters, however, contained this admonition: "Beloved Brother Heath will take heed to the time, when he reads my journal, that greater matters may not give place to it—I mean the worship of God and the ministration of the Word. If portions be read on a Friday evening, or if need be on a Monday evening, the rest may be read in private at leisure." Chapman would not permit news of himself to intrude on the more important business of God's Word.

Chapman had a very active week in Cork. He visited

the Anglican parish rector who had established the orphanage, and wrote favorably in his letters of their time together. He conferred with leaders in the Lord's work, visited sick wards, and even preached at a funeral. "Yesterday forenoon," he wrote, "I visited the sick, and expounded the Scriptures in the room of one of the sufferers to a little company of believers of every name. Alas, that we should have needed by our divisions, any but our proper titles." Formal divisions among Christians grieved Chapman, but he never hesitated to minister to all groups in his efforts to demonstrate the unity of all believers.

A map of Chapman's long walk around Ireland.

On Sunday afternoon, after much prayer he preached outdoors for the first time in Ireland, in one of the poorest sections of Cork. This was a new event to the inhabitants. Chapman wrote:

> After a little while a crowd of boys, set on by the men, raised a yell and sought to drown my voice: one man said, "Speak without the Bible," meaning well, for if Roman Catholics hear the Scriptures read by a Protestant, they must confess to the priest this their sin. I could not, however, put away the Bible, out of which I was reading the 19th of John. I prayed aloud before I left the ground, and to hear prayer from a Protestant is in their eyes a sin; my praying for them made them very angry. Then the crowd of boys followed me and other brethren that were with me, yelling through the streets a good distance; their violence, however, was restrained to cries and mocking; my own spirit was full of peace in God and pity and prayer for them.

Chapman was not discouraged by the angry reception; rather the fact that he was not forcibly removed gave him hope for the rest of the trip. An angry reception, he believed, was often better than indifference.

While in Cork he also visited J. M. Code. Code, like Darby, was a graduate of Trinity College, had been ordained in the Church of England, and had left the Anglican church during the early 1830s for reasons of conscience. After that, Code had taught and evangelized independently in the area around Cork and he became a leader in the Assembly that had started there. Thus Chapman was anxious to meet him and discuss views on church unity and Darby's action in Plymouth. In his gracious style Chapman wrote:

> I have had some sweet converse also with Brother Code on matters of difference of judgment between us; we rejoiced in our unity, as far as we discerned it, and judged it a cause of self-humiliation that we

could not fully agree, but not a reason for strife and separation. God would soon make His children one, did they always set their faces...towards the mercy-seat.

So both humble men remained in unity, although they disagreed on a fundamental issue. Two or three years later Code moved to Bath, England, where he continued his ministry. Remarkably people from the Church of England would come to the chapel in Bath to hear him preach. If he was partial to Darby's views when Chapman visited him at Cork, he had changed since, for in Bath he took a more open stance toward all believers.

Chapman also wrote of his concern about the influence of Roman Catholicism:

The Roman Catholics here, both priests and people, are very far above those of Spain; there both deride their own religion and scoff at all religion; here, a false religion (which is yet not pure error but the truth corrupted and perverted) is ignorantly held in reverence. I found in Spain indifference and scorn; here is a vexed and troubled conscience seeking rest and not knowing how to obtain it. I reckon myself favored of God to speak to such consciences.

Chapman was no doubt somewhat relieved by what he was finding in Ireland, but ignorance of the truths in God's Word is serious wherever it is found.

His itinerary next took him westward from Cork through the famine-stricken villages and countryside of southwestern Ireland. Now he saw the devastation first-hand and was not surprised to learn that desperately poor people would commit theft in order to obtain food and lodging in jail. His first stop was the town of Mallow, a short day's walk from Cork. At the house of his host he found letters from Henry Heath and Bessie Paget awaiting him. He stayed in Mallow several days and on Sunday again preached outdoors, knowing that this was the only way most people could be reached with the gospel:

96

The poor people, just come out from hearing mass, flocked around me and, if some mocked, most were attentive; [my host] told me that certain of them who kept others quiet were men of bad character; likewise several heard from their windows....I praise God for bringing me to Mallow....I believe God has set before me an open door and that none can shut it; thus you see your prayers for me answered....Oh, beloved brethren and sisters, how great is your favor and power with God! Use that favor and power.

Chapman's vision for Ireland remained constantly before him. "I am continually comparing my present lot with my solitary journeyings in Spain," he wrote, "and praising God for the lamp He has lighted up here; yet I pray that many may be raised up to preach out of doors." His heart went out to the Irish people, and he saw that the spreading of the gospel in Ireland was best accomplished in the village squares or streets, where the people could be reached. While penning the lines we just read, he learned that Darby had become quite ill, and he ended his letter with this postscript: "We have had prayer for beloved brother Darby. The Lord grant us his restoration to health. His name is very dear to children of God in Ireland." Chapman seems to have harbored no anger or resentment toward the man who was taking the movement in directions with which he could not agree.

As it turned out, Chapman's visit to Mallow had great impact. Some weeks after Chapman's stay there, a penniless and unemployed youth became seriously ill and was brought to the Mallow workhouse. Told of his dangerous condition, he was asked if he would like to see a priest. He replied that he had heard a stranger preach Christ in the marketplace on a Sunday and that the Savior was all-sufficient for him. Possessing this faith, he died. Chapman learned of this only much later; a person in ministry often does not see the fruit of his or her labor, but God's Word does not return to Him void (Isaiah 55:11).

After leaving Mallow, Chapman set out toward the west where the famine had hit hardest. As he walked in the cold rain, he saw a devastated countryside in despair. In a small village Chapman spoke at the children's workhouse and visited poor families. He then wrote:

> There are 1800 in the poorhouses of Kanturk, besides many thousands receiving out-door relief. The Lord Himself must help. It is a great mercy that a penny procures a pound of Indian meal, and that turf [peat, used for fuel] is plentiful. Thus I have great comfort in distributing alms and have not seen a cottage without a fire. I have heard from eye-witnesses such tales of the misery and death that reigned during the famine as I hope not to forget.... The land looks desolate, but the inhabitants have made it so, how barren, how dreary and gloomy the state of their souls!

Chapman carried with him a quantity of halfpence, which he gave to destitute people whom he met as he walked. He used his almsgiving to initiate conversations, not just to alleviate hunger. "When...I gave a small sum to a farmer's wife to distribute among the poor in her neighborhood," he wrote, "she said, 'May the Almighty God and the Almighty Virgin Mary bless you.'" In a letter Chapman remarked on this language, which placed the mother of Jesus on a par with God, but he probably made no comment to the well-meaning woman. "Still," he wrote, "Ireland is better than Spain. Superstition is better than profane irreligion. Conscience speaks here and afflicts men with dread of death, and generally they hear me with reverence when preaching Christ."

The money Chapman distributed, which no doubt came from Christians at Bear Street Chapel, was a pittance compared to what was needed, and the people's despair only added to the desolation of their environment. Nevertheless the light of the gospel was there. "The gospel is, however, preached in the [Anglican] Church at Kanturk; I visited and prayed with the young clergyman there." Again we see Chapman's spirit of Christian unity and willingness to cross denominational lines.

Although Chapman preached to the poor, several of

his hosts in Ireland were wealthy. In a letter to Barnstaple, Chapman wrote:

> Let none think that the distress of Ireland is only the poor man's lot; more of hunger and bodily want may be the poor man's portion, but he either owes no debts or is not expected to pay; he can go into the poor-house and be no gazing-stock; but the rich man...must meet demands, old and new, upon his purse...and thus with straitened means he becomes in mind and heart burdened and careworn as the poor man cannot be. Let, therefore, saints in England in their prayers for Ireland not forget the rich when they pray for the poor.

Although he had given away his fortune and had no fixed income, Chapman did not believe that all of God's children must do the same. Chapman's chosen lifestyle of poverty was a covenant between himself and God. He did not press it upon his friends.

The town of Tralee on the southwestern coast was Chapman's next contact point. There he planned to stay with friends and pick up his mail. A long day's walk in stormy weather along a river valley brought him to the small village of Castleisland. The next day he walked over a mountain pass and down into Tralee. His host, Sir Edward Denny, was gaining prominence among the Brethren. Chapman had much in common with Sir Edward. Each had been born into a wealthy family and each had a poet's heart. An obituary notice fifty years later said of Denny: "Nearly the whole town of Tralee belonged to him. He had an opportunity...of raising his rents to figures that, in some cases, would not have been considered extortionate had they been quadrupled. He however decided to accept the old rates." During the year that Chapman visited, Denny published *Hymns and Poems,* a work that became well known. Greatly interested in prophetic questions, Denny later published many charts depicting the events prophesied for the endtimes. These charts became popular and were widely used in Britain for many years.

"I well remember dear Mr. Chapman's coming to Tralee to see my father and mother," wrote a daughter of the Dennys years later. "He asked me if he should mark some verses in my Bible. I was very pleased and got the book at once, and he marked the 13th, 14th, and 15th verses of the 15th chapter of St. John. I was quite a child; he also marked Psalm 27:4 and 11." Chapman loved children and always sought them out when visiting someone's home. Whether he stayed at an inn or in a home with servants, he made a point of discussing Christ with those who helped him.

After resting at Tralee, Chapman continued northward, arriving in two days at the village of Tarbert at the mouth of the Shannon river. "I reached Tarbert," he wrote, "in time for a meeting (appointed without notice of my coming) of Roman Catholics to read the Scriptures." He did not hesitate to bring the Word of God to any group and on this day he preached on the quay at Tarbert while awaiting the river steamer to Limerick, some forty miles east.

Chapman spent five days in pleasant fellowship with Christians at Limerick, but instead of relaxing he spoke each day at various schools and to several groups of adults. In England he had a firm rule of relaxing on Saturdays, but on this trip he seems to have set that aside. He felt the urgency of the Lord's business.

From Limerick he journeyed northeastward up the valley of the Shannon river, stopping to preach in the villages. Chapman was now in the center of Ireland. Finding some Christian workers whom he knew, he stayed in that vicinity for five days, encouraging and helping them. He then prepared to walk again, but a Christian worker recognized that Chapman had become weary and conveyed him the next thirty miles in a one-horse gig. They passed through several villages and arrived at the town of Ballinasloe. Tired, Chapman wrote back to Barnstaple:

> I am humbled to think that I passed [a crowd] without addressing them, and without asking of God whether I should speak or hold my peace. My strength, that is, my spiritual strength, needed

recruiting....I might have found especial help from God by looking to Him. I did not enquire of Him, but pressed forward, hoping to meet others further on. I met none.

More days of walking and preaching followed as Chapman headed toward Westport on the western coast. The last day of this stretch was difficult. Chapman walked forty miles in one day "with strong wind in my face the whole way, and rain, snow, and hail every now and then. I asked the Lord to turn the wind, but His answer for that day was that His grace sufficed me, so I was happy in Him and preached His Word to a few on the way....My hope of seeing brethren in the Lord, none of whom I had ever seen before, spurred me on, and in a few minutes after I arrived...I forgot fatigue." Not many men would have had the physical endurance or the will to accomplish what he did. Probably able to hire a coach, he determined to walk the roads in order to meet people. The next day was Sunday; Chapman wrote:

We had a precious meeting...for breaking bread. In the afternoon there was fine weather, and I preached in the Square with little interruption; the greater number heard me gladly. One struck me on the ear and temples with a football, but another (a Roman Catholic) besought me to use her handkerchief to wipe off the mark. In the evening I preached to many at the meeting-room of the brethren.

Much of his interaction throughout his trip was with children, and his time in Westport was no different. "On Monday afternoon...I addressed a goodly company of children together with their parents and others....I had joy in it, yet I thought of Brother Heath and longed for him. The Lord direct his steps to Ireland, where he is greatly needed and would be dearly welcomed." Henry Heath never did go to Ireland to labor, and moved later that year to the countryside north of London to work among poor people there.

Chapman was now in the sixth week of his trip. In Westport he met with Charles H. Mackintosh, well known later by the initials *CHM* with which he signed his many expository works. Mackintosh had been converted after reading one of Darby's booklets and was running a day school. Fearing that he was becoming too enthusiastic in his school work, Mackintosh later quit it to devote all his time to expository writing and ministering the Word. Chapman surely discussed the situation at Plymouth with Mackintosh, who remained loyal to Darby's views, but recorded nothing of it.

Chapman then walked on, preaching at too many villages to recount here. At Tubbercurry, J. Butler Stoney came over from the town of Boyle, where he labored in a desolate district, in order to confer with Chapman. Together they ministered for a few days in the mountainous area around Tubbercurry. A dozen years younger than Chapman, Stoney was zealously evangelistic and a staunch Darby supporter. Nevertheless he came to respect Chapman greatly during the few days they had together, so much so that he pleaded with Chapman to return with him to Boyle for further mutual labor. Chapman, however, felt obliged to refuse; his own itinerary took priority.

At Sligo, a good-sized town on Sligo bay in northwestern Ireland, Chapman's mind was diverted to events back in England. Mail carried disturbing news (perhaps also mentioned by Stoney): the unrest at Plymouth had affected Bethesda Chapel in Bristol. Chapman wanted to return, but felt his greater responsibility still lay in Ireland. "I cannot as yet fix the time of my return," he wrote, "but desire, in common with many others, a solemn meeting of brethren for prayer to be held about the third week next month [April]. 'Behold, I come quickly.'"

Next he walked northeast into Ulster, which now is Northern Ireland. There his encounters included preaching and reading the Scriptures with a group of Wesleyans. As he approached Londonderry on the northern tip of the country, weariness again set in, so he caught a train for the last few miles to the city. He then wrote:

On the Lord's Day, after breaking bread with a little band of believers at their room, I preached out of doors on the quay; the interruption was only for a few minutes from some boys, and that arose from a hearer's dealing not according to Christ with a boy who in jest offered me a penny. Indeed, I must say that my chief difficulties in out-of-door preaching have been occasioned by friends who did not understand, or did not remember, that it was my glory to suffer for Christ's sake, and who therefore have dealt with my revilers not with the mind and contrary to the precept of Christ. I pray God that my brethren may consider this.

Chapman became ill that evening after preaching at another meeting and was forced to spend a few days in bed. Yet he began preaching again on Thursday and, with two local laborers for the Lord, he ministered the remainder of the week in the Londonderry area. The people of Ulster are mainly of English or Scottish descent. Gaelic, or Irish as it is also called, was not so commonly spoken there as in the lower parts of Ireland. During the first part of his journey Chapman often expressed the desire to learn Gaelic in order to be more effective. Now he wrote:

But little Irish is heard in Ulster except in certain mountainous parts, and I would here say that while the gift of speaking in Irish is a very precious one, yet the field is very large and daily growing larger for those who speak English only....As for myself I have had no time for learning Irish, and I judge it better for me to be praying for those who have the tongue and preach in it than to be myself learning it.

On April 1, still weak from his illness, Chapman left Londonderry. He stopped at a village just a few miles away and preached there for several days. When he resumed his journey, he hurried through Belfast and headed south, determined to reach Dublin on the appointed day. "I was obliged to use conveyances," he wrote, "but, oh, how much rather do I choose to travel on foot for the work of the Lord, and communion with Him." On some stretches he still walked, but he wearily confessed in his next letter that "a poor man whom I overtook a little way from Dunleer offered to carry my knapsack, and for the first time since I came to Ireland I parted with it to another. He was a Roman Catholic, and told me that he had twice been compelled by the priests to put away the New Testament, which he had taken pleasure in reading."

Chapman arrived in Dublin on time but refused to rest except on Sunday morning when he attended a larger Assembly on Brunswick Street, where between two and three hundred broke bread. He spoke briefly outdoors in the afternoon and preached in the evening "at the Room." The Brunswick Street Chapel operated a number of schools for children and, true to form, Chapman addressed those children on Monday and preached in a schoolhouse that evening. But on Tuesday a nurse was called to examine the exhausted man. She prescribed the obvious cure: rest.

After conversing with the leaders of the Assemblies in the Dublin area for several more days, Chapman returned to England. He went first to Liverpool and rested a few days with the family of his brother John. Then he traveled down to Bristol to review the situation at Bethesda Chapel. He stayed only a day, knowing that he would soon return on what would likely be unpleasant business. For now, he just wanted to get home, and on April 21 he reached Barnstaple.

In Ireland Chapman had ministered to the rich as well as to the poor. He had encouraged believers in large and small Assemblies. He had interacted with Anglicans, Roman Catholics, Presbyterians, and Wesleyans as well as with Brethren. He had counseled leaders concerning a growing split in what had been for fifteen years a harmonious movement. He had ministered across the whole country during a period of three months and his impact was significant. The extent of that impact cannot be gauged now, but in light of the religious revival that swept all of Ireland eleven years after his visit, Chapman may well have been one of the instruments God used to prepare the country.

13
Attempt at a Reconciliation

The two years preceding Chapman's trip through Ireland, and the months to follow, were times of pain for him as he observed acquaintances and dear friends engage in most un-Christian conduct. Never one to force his opinions on others, he now felt compelled to confront antagonists in an effort to reverse a growing split and save a new and promising movement of which he was a part. Any church leader who has gone through the heartaches and soul-searching of a church split knows the agony that follows in its wake. In order to understand this conflict and the context in which it took place, let us review some historical facts and trends.

The congregations of Christians that sprang up in England and Ireland during the late 1820s and 1830s did not all share the same attitudes, even though they were joined by strong bonds. Each had to address and settle such issues as style of worship and instruction, local leadership, and relationships to other churches. There was, however, surprising uniformity concerning worship, hymnody, and preaching within the Assemblies during their earliest days. Weekly observance of the Lord's Supper was universal, for example. The rediscovery of a Christian's freedom to celebrate this memorial feast without clergy gave this observance a special significance. It became a symbol of the new movement. The congregations also used many hymns in common. Chapman, Darby, Sir Edward Denny, and many others actively wrote new hymns, particularly hymns that were appropriate for the Lord's Supper.

In the earliest days of the movement, preaching was based solely on the Bible and was provided only by gifted, educated men. B. W. Newton and J. L. Harris, and to a lesser extent Henry Soltau, preached at Plymouth, since Percy Hall and George Wigram had left to establish new works in other parts of England and Darby was a traveler. Müller and Craik alternated preaching at Bethesda and Gideon Chapels. Chapman did most of the preaching at Ebenezer and Bear Street Chapels.

Local leadership, however, developed diversely among the different Assemblies. A few years after their formation, the churches at Barnstaple and Bristol espoused the concept of a recognized plural leadership vested in spiritually qualified men. Churches in which Darby was influential adopted the attitude that leaders should not be formally identified. To them, all men in good standing had more or less equal footing.

Darby, believing that God was rejecting organized denominations, also began asserting that Christians should separate themselves from such organizations. Although Chapman, Groves, Müller, Craik, and quite a few other Assembly leaders were unhappy with the practices of many denominations, they did not share Darby's separatist views.

Another issue surfaced concerning the relationships among the Assemblies. Many Assembly leaders, including most of those from the original Dublin groups (with the notable exception of Lord Congleton), came to believe that unity required a strong interdependence. The principal men of this biography held that interactions among the Assemblies were useful, but that no Assembly or group of Assemblies should be able to dictate the actions of any other. Each Assembly was responsible to Christ alone. They further felt liberty to interact freely with all individuals or groups who they believed were sound in the major doctrines, even though agreement on all points could not be reached.

Perhaps it was inevitable that a movement encompassing such divergent views on unity and leadership would divide. As commonly happens, one event triggered a bigger event. The trigger in this case was a clash between the powerful personalities of Newton and Darby. Only a year or so after they formed the new church at Plymouth, these men discovered that they differed on many points, including prophecy and leadership. Newton, who argued that a single identified leader was preferable, implied that he should be that person in the Plymouth Assembly. In practice he already was, and even Darby had promoted that belief at the beginning.

In contrast to Newton's role in Plymouth, Darby's ministry was largely itinerant. He traveled almost constantly throughout England and Ireland and spent many years in Switzerland and France. Thus the Assembly at Plymouth came increasingly under Newton's influence. This was by no means bad, at least during the first decade. The congregation grew quickly and its spirit of evangelism was strong. The people were well-versed in the Bible, so much so that the Plymouth church—in sharp contrast to other area churches—gained a reputation throughout South Devon as a company of Bible experts.

During his travels Darby promoted his ideas on prophecy and church structure. But during Darby's absence, Newton began a campaign of trying to steer some of the Assemblies in Devon and neighboring Somerset away from Darby's ideas. When Darby returned from Europe in 1845, he saw what was happening and realized that if the movement were going to follow the path he believed was essential, Newton's influence had to be checked. As it turned out, Newton's personality gave Darby a needed weapon.

Although gracious, studious, well educated, and a gifted preacher, Newton had developed a certain arrogance and a critical spirit. Consequently many people in the Plymouth Assembly were growing restless under his leadership. One Plymouth leader, Sir Alexander Campbell, left in 1845 because of Newton's style, and J. L. Harris—Newton's principal copreacher—also had problems with him. Consider the words Newton wrote of Robert Chapman a few years later:

> And so with Robert Chapman. He never did receive prophetic truth. For years he rejected the idea of the Millennium altogether—wouldn't listen to it, and then accepted it merely as a notion, and now cultivates poverty as a grace....I remember his coming to me. I wasn't well off myself, but he was worse; he had been walking about all day having had no food but a loaf they had found on a common in answer to prayer. That sort of thing. Once I remember he went to a physician who had come to the meetings, whose wife was a Christian—he went to their house, enquired for the servant, had tea in the kitchen with the cook, and never asked for the lady. This as a sort of Christian testimony to lowly mindedness.

Chapman was most willing to support Newton during his growing tribulations, but Newton could not understand Chapman. He also expressed critical sentiments about George Müller, the wealthy Sir Alexander Campbell, and Lord Congleton. Although they did not adopt Chapman's lifestyle of poverty, Campbell and Congleton ignored class distinctions and promoted the breakdown of class barriers as Chapman did. Newton did not agree with their position.

By 1845 the Christians at Plymouth, who in former days had been so eager and evangelistic, had lost much of their happy fellowship. Darby saw this and in mid-1845 let it be known that he planned to set up a new Assembly in Plymouth. Darby's action was welcomed by many and deplored by many. Harris, who had parted with Newton, sided with Darby. Soltau, Campbell, and some other leaders sided with Newton.

When the Brethren in other towns learned of Darby's intent, many of them became alarmed. Lord Congleton— no supporter of Newton—strenuously objected. Chapman was convinced that patience and confession of pride before God could resolve all the problems. The ill will being expressed among the brothers at Plymouth was certainly not Christlike, but divergence of opinion within the local church was not new to Chapman. He had encountered it when he first came to Ebenezer Chapel. At that time he had used great patience while instructing the church, and after a time the congregation had essentially become unified. Why wouldn't such an approach work at Plymouth?

Chapman viewed the problem principally as that of reconciling two difficult personalities; Darby viewed the problem as that of directing the movement he was so actively promoting. Chapman was thinking locally; Darby was thinking globally. Citing his experiences with disunity, Chapman spoke with Darby toward the end of 1845, probably in Plymouth, and urged him not to proceed with his intentions. Chapman probably met with Newton too during this visit. Perhaps this is the visit that Newton commented on in his earlier-mentioned letter. If it is, Chapman's visit had little effect on Newton.

Darby refused to heed Chapman's advice and said, "I will go out and whoever will may follow me." By the end of 1845 he set up a new Assembly, but he probably grossly miscalculated the effect of his action. He must have assumed that most people would quickly leave the Newton Assembly, thus isolating Newton. Instead, two Assemblies in Plymouth of about equal size were at odds with each other. More important, the split caused confusion and unhappiness in more than these two churches. Prior to this split the closely knit Assemblies throughout Britain and Ireland had tended to think of themselves as one body; now they were being asked to choose sides.

Chapman decided that he should take an active role in what was happening at Plymouth. His attempt at avoiding a split had not succeeded, so he determined that the next best thing to do would be to promote healing. The people needed to learn that their willful actions had been against the spirit of Christ. Consulting with several leaders, Chapman convinced them that a day of prayer and confession was needed. If the people would acknowledge their sinful attitudes, perhaps reconciliation could result. Chapman sent a circular letter dated January 1846 to all the churches with which he was acquainted. It was both a scolding and a call to repentance. He wrote:

> Certain Brethren in the Lord in different parts of the kingdom having agreed to set apart the second Wednesday of the next month for prayer and humiliation, on account of the divisions in the Church of Christ, it is proposed to all to whom those divisions are a grief to join in the above service. If, as is commonly confessed, the present low estate of the people of God be the bitter fruit of their having so long time grieved the Spirit of God, then is it not the highest aggravation of their guilt that they have so little mourned, either jointly or singly, publicly or privately, for grieving the Holy Ghost?...In the meekness and gentleness of Christ, it is urged upon the consciences of saints to consider especially the dishonor done to God by different opinions and judgments among His children....Different degrees of attainment in grace and knowledge, and differences in gifts and offices, must of necessity have place among the members of Christ; but such diversity is of God, and works unity; contrarieties of judgment concerning the truth always check the fellowship of saints, and, if not mourned before God, gender strife and division.

Not only did many of the Assemblies reject this letter; they criticized Chapman for having sent it. To them, Darby had acted in good conscience so there was no cause for acknowledgment of sin and no need for public repentance.

Chapman had twice failed. What seemed so clear to him—that Christians were not acting in Christ's love, that confession before God of willfulness was a necessary first step to reconciliation—was not even comprehended by those he loved so much.

Now it was only a matter of time before the inevitable conclusion. In 1847 Harris, Darby, and others became aware that some of Newton's ten-year-old writings, which denounced a growing heresy called Irvingism, contained statements that could be interpreted as impugning the sinless humanity of Christ. Since about 1835 the scholarly Newton had attempted to address the difficult question of Christ's humanity and its implications. Biblical scholars agreed that Christ was "very God and very man," but as a man and as a Jew under the law, to what extent did the curse on Adam fall upon Jesus, if at all? (It was the question that had stumbled Irving, and in a few more years it would cause trouble for Darby when he wrote about the sufferings of Christ.)

When the offending statements and their logical conclusions were brought to Newton's attention, he recognized his errors and withdrew them publicly and in writing. This demonstrated considerable courage. Darby and his colleagues, however, believed that Newton's reversal was not genuine and they influenced most of the Assemblies in South Devon to exclude the Newton Assembly from their circle of fellowship. Newton's sympathizers, they believed, should not be welcomed among them because they had been contaminated with an evil doctrine. This fear and suspicion of fellow Christians, obsession with spiritual purity, and absence of love was not of course unique in church history. It was a sad reflection of many other groups, such as the Walkerites and Kellyites in Ireland and the Sandemanians in England and Scotland, who also started on the path of spiritual purity but were diverted by fears that overrode love.

Darby had won. Newton recognized defeat and left Plymouth for good in December 1847. Soltau and three other leaders of the original Plymouth Assembly, in great agony of heart, apologized for having supported Newton's teachings. Soltau remained in Plymouth only a few more months, then moved his family to the town of Exmouth near Exeter—away from his humiliation, away from the hard feelings, away from the controversy.

By April 1848 the controversy had engulfed Bethesda Chapel in Bristol. One of the Plymouth families that had sided with Newton had moved to Bristol and applied for fellowship at Bethesda Chapel. After an interview in which the family members asserted that they did not agree with the errors of Newton, they were admitted. This caused much uncertainty among the Bethesda people about whether the right decision had been made and of course Darby's Assembly in Plymouth was greatly upset.

Chapman returned from his missionary tour through Ireland about this time and Groves had returned from India. Both of them became involved in the controversy. Leaders from several Assemblies near Bristol decided to convene a meeting at nearby Bath in May to try to analyze Newton's writings and, if possible, to suggest a path toward reconciliation. The majority of those present, including Müller and Chapman, concluded that the writings of Newton, although they were difficult to understand and sometimes seemed self-contradictory, contained serious error. Craik, who because of his scholarly inclination and experience was probably better able than the rest to assess Newton's writings, delayed an opinion. To his mind, many of Newton's statements were so ambiguous as to defy analysis.

The Bethesda elders realized that they needed to explain their reasons for admitting the former supporters of Newton and did so in writing, but Darby and his supporters rejected their explanation. At Darby's urging, many Assemblies throughout Britain excluded Bethesda from their circle of fellowship and had nothing further to do with Assemblies or individuals who supported Bethesda. Thus the Brethren divided into two camps.

Shortly after Darby's exclusion of Bethesda, he came to Bristol to talk with Müller about the whole matter. Was he ready to offer some way of reconciliation? We'll never know, for Müller angrily refused to talk to him and they never met again. The seemingly unending chain reaction still had not run its course. Müller, acting quite out of character, had given in to the human impulse to retaliate and soon the gentle Craik did likewise. George Wigram, Darby's principal lieutenant in the Newton dealings, had circulated a letter severely criticizing Craik for delaying a repudiation of Newton's teaching. Craik's thoughtful reply did not satisfy Wigram, who continued his diatribe. Exasperated, Craik issued a statement saying that he considered himself separated from all the "exclusive" Brethren.

Chapman left nothing in writing about his feelings concerning the actions of these two dear friends, but they surely grieved him deeply. He was certainly opposed to the personal attacks in which Darby, Wigram, and others had recently indulged, but his response was to reply only in love. Chapman was probably viewed as naive and hopelessly idealistic—someone who did not understand the realities of human nature. But understanding human nature all too well, he knew it was possible for Christian brothers to repent and see their failings, if only they would seek the face of God. All the rest was only an excuse.

Since the various Assemblies similar to those at Barnstaple and Bristol were largely independent anyway, one may ask, "Why was this exclusion by the others so troublesome?" People such as Chapman were greatly disturbed by such an action, viewing it as a device of Satan to break a movement that had seen much fruit and experienced great freedom of worship. Interaction between likeminded fellowships had been sweet. Now Christians who had formerly been on good terms were at odds. One who had been in the original Plymouth Assembly wrote later, "It was too fair a scene for Satan to contemplate, and he must by some means mar its beauties and desolate its loveliness."

Several people on both sides were unhappy about what had happened and made continued attempts at reconciliation, but to no avail. A meeting of twelve influential Brethren from all over the country—all prominent figures in the movement and many outside the immediate conflict—was again convened at Bath to consider the whole issue. During this meeting Chapman, challenging Darby, said, "You should have waited longer before separating" (referring to Darby's inability to resolve his conflict with Newton and his 1845 action).

"I waited six months," Darby replied defensively.

Chapman's reply was uncharacteristically testy: "But if it had been at Barnstaple, we should have waited six years."

The conveners of the Bath meeting had hoped that their combined influence could convince the Christians who sided with Darby that Bethesda and the Assemblies sympathetic to it were not slackening in their resolve against fundamental error. But the document they published had no healing effect. Chapman grieved over this development but was helpless to do anything further. He was even reviled by some of the brothers who were sympathetic to Darby. Assemblies where he had once been welcome now refused him fellowship. Darby, however, defended Chapman. When some of Darby's followers tried to argue that Chapman was deficient in some doctrinal basics, Darby reproved them, saying, "You leave that man alone; he lives what I teach." On another occasion Darby said, "We talk of the heavenlies, but Robert Chapman lives in them."

Darby's personality offers us an unsettling look into ourselves. His personality may have been drawn with bolder strokes, but it is easy for us to catch a glimpse of ourselves in him. He was vicious and un-Christlike when crossed, but loving and gracious at other times. As we do, he probably excused his actions by claiming that he had done only what had to be done. Yet he lacked the balance between love and firmness that Chapman so well exhibited.

Chapman refused to use disparaging language when speaking of Christian brothers and sisters who followed Darby. Although some people began to use less than gracious terms for them, Chapman referred to them as "brethren dearly beloved and longed for" (Philippians 4:1). His sorrow was genuine. There was no sense of "good riddance" on his part. He had no sense of relief to be done with those who had opposed him and would have no further Christian fellowship with him. These were his "brethren whose consciences lead them to refuse my fellowship and to deprive me of theirs." His love for Darby continued unabated too. Many years later some "open" Brethren leaders were at a conference in Leominster when word came that Darby had died. Chapman arose to request that those present sing one of the hymns written by Darby, "Rest of the Saints Above."

The Newton-Darby split, which never was healed, plagued and grieved Chapman his entire life. An exclusive Assembly that formed in Barnstaple sometime after the split caused much unhappiness among Christians there. The exclusive Assembly reviled Chapman and accused the open Assembly at Bear Street Chapel of harboring or being sympathetic with heretics. Through it all, however, Chapman managed to maintain a spirit of love among the Christians at Bear Street. He never retaliated. With prayer and a loving, longing spirit, he pursued those who opposed him, always hoping for reconciliation.

Chapman's role in the attempted reconciliation brought him to the forefront of the movement. During the following years he was often asked to visit Assemblies where there were problems and his advice was listened to with respect. His firm, loving, and tactful ways of dealing with groups of people won him much admiration. He was careful not to show impatience or anger, but only expressed sorrow and love for those whose actions were in opposition to himself or, in his judgment, to Christ.

Consider a letter that Chapman wrote to Edward Cronin, a founder of a Dublin group in the 1820s. Cronin had joined Norris Groves for a time as a missionary in Baghdad, but when Darby called on all Assemblies to have nothing to do with Christians attending Bethesda Chapel or with anyone who sympathized with them, Cronin complied and wrote to Groves that he could have nothing further to do with him. Distressed, Groves pleaded with Cronin, but to no avail. All communications between them ceased. In 1881, however, Cronin was himself excommunicated from an exclusive Assembly because of his efforts to resolve a problem elsewhere. Chapman then wrote to him with a heart of love: "Hearing that you are in the Lord's furnace, I cannot but bear burdens with you....We rise above all that may seem to us to blame in others, be they our brethren in Christ or of the world....The faults of others we mourn, because of the Spirit, the Comforter, being grieved." The trials of others were the trials of Chapman. In a letter dated 1887 he wrote, "The pressures of the times on many faithful children of God are well known to me, and I am with them in the furnace."

At one point a leader of Bear Street Chapel was accused of teaching an unscriptural doctrine similar to that which Newton had espoused. A letter written in 1869 to Chapman asked whether this could be so. Chapman's reply was firm, but his anguish shows through:

> Oh, that we, yea, all saints, might be moved each one to prove himself before God....Our answer to your enquiry is, first, that if anyone seek our fellowship here after having listened to such teaching, whether he come from the one party or the other (we hold both parties alike dear to us as our fellow-members in Christ our Head), such an one must be judged according to the Word of God and the rule of Christ. Cases differing must not be confounded. If anyone bring the evil doctrine...his welfare and his healing would be sought by brethren here...but to fellowship he would not be received....Then as to the particular case you mentioned, we have exercised godly jealousy and find that the evil doctrine is not held by the brother you name....May we and all saints cease to grieve the Spirit of God....Shall we not then have the joy of seeing the self-judged flowing together from all quarters.

On another occasion Chapman wrote, "I have frequently been severely tried in my faith, but the Lord in His own gracious time has sent the means." What seems to be unanswered prayer may produce a great trial of faith. It seemed to Chapman that his prayers for reconciliation of his fellow pioneers had gone unanswered, but he frequently said, "Our Father knows all about it," and this sustained him.

Chapman's second missionary trip to Spain.

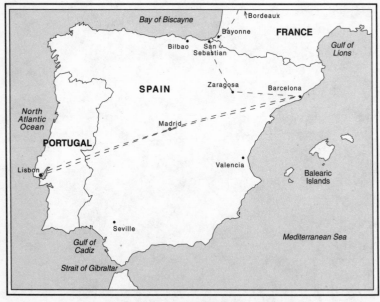

Chapman's third missionary trip to Spain.

14
The Constant Evangelist

R obert Chapman often talked about Spain in his sermons and it was always in his prayers. The events of
his missionary trip of 1838 remained vivid in his mind,
and his burden for the Spanish people who were kept ignorant of the Scriptures did not diminish with the passage
of time. The religious situation in Spain improved only
slightly during the two decades after 1838. Although the
outcry of several countries in the 1850s over the incarcera-
tion and exile of the young Spanish evangelist Matamoros
had forced the Spanish government to be more lenient
toward Protestantism, Spain was still officially closed to
evangelistic intervention.

THE SECOND MISSIONARY TRIP

In the early 1860s Chapman looked for an opportune
time to return to Spain. Bessie Paget, his constant
helper at Bear Street Chapel and in the ministries at New

Buildings Street, was elderly and had not been well for some years, so Chapman did not want to leave her for an extended period. But after she died in 1863, Chapman prepared for his second missionary visit to Spain.

God had also been laying the Spanish people on the hearts of W. Gould, G. Lawrence, and their wives, all of whom lived in the Barnstaple area. When Chapman announced his travel plans, they committed before God to go to Spain as permanent missionaries. Since Spain still prohibited overt missionary activity, the five arranged to establish a printing business there and left England together at the end of 1863.

The small party also had a mission en route to Spain. Chapman had learned that a number of Spaniards who had been exiled because of their non-Catholic stance now lived in Bordeaux, France. Christians in France had welcomed and clothed the exiles when they first arrived, but the lot of the exiles was hard. Most of them either had no employment or very meager incomes. They did not know whether they could ever return to their homeland and they needed encouragement. Many Christians in Britain had given money so the Chapman group could buy clothes for the exiles. So the missionaries stayed in Bordeaux several days, ministering to these poor people, praying with them, and preaching the gospel.

Next the five missionaries traveled south to Bayonne on the coast of France near the border of Spain, where Manuel Matamoros was living in exile. After praying with Matamoros, Chapman discussed his own plans for preaching and evangelizing in Spain. No doubt the young Spaniard was able to advise Chapman on many points. Frail as a result of his imprisonments, Matamoros died not long afterward, having the conviction that the gospel would soon be preached throughout Spain.

The group then entered Bilbao on the northern coast of Spain and found that the Spaniards now felt a little freer to listen to the gospel. Chapman wrote:

> The work is opening upon us here by little and little; and "who has despised the day of small things?"...

The Church of Rome has lost her dominion as to the conscience of the greater part of the people, although still upheld by the law of the land; but those who despise the Church of Rome have nothing better before their eyes.

This was the real dilemma of Spain. The evangelical church was scattered and underground; most people were ignorant of it and did not know how or where to find Biblical instruction.

The Goulds and Lawrences decided to live in Barcelona on the east coast of Spain. The sixty-year-old Chapman stayed with them a short while as they began their printing business, which would provide a base from which they could evangelize. When they were established, he embarked on his missionary journey, traveling north to south and east to west across the country, both walking and traveling by coach. He also journeyed into Portugal, talking to people as he went along and seeking out and encouraging a few Christians whom he knew.

An interesting incident shows the constant evangelist at work. A man in Spain as a pioneer representative of a missionary society was traveling by stagecoach to the city of Seville. Finding himself seated next to a man who quietly commenced to read his Bible, he recorded these words:

> I soon introduced myself, and quickly found that we were on the same errand. And as I had travelled far and wide in many lands, I proffered my services as travelling companion. Mr. Chapman at once expressed his thanks and handed me his purse; this greatly took me by surprise, and I thought I was in the company of a very good man, but a little "touched in his upper story." On our arrival in Seville, we were surrounded by a crowd, and a man demanded money to convey our luggage to the hotel. This was provided for in the funds already paid, so I stoutly resisted the imposition.
>
> In the midst of the altercation I felt a hand gently

tapping me on the shoulder, and, as I turned, Mr. Chapman said, "Pay the man the money."

Hotly I replied, "Indeed, Mr. Chapman, I shall not. Here is your purse, and you can do as you like, but I won't be taken in like that."

Never shall I forget the scene which followed. Quickly taking from his purse the amount demanded, Mr. Chapman took the man's hand in his, and, as he placed the money in it, told him he was quite aware that it was an imposition, but that he had come to his country to tell the glad tidings of salvation, that "God so loved the world that He gave his only begotten Son." The money must have burned in the man's hand as he stood there and listened to the Gospel story.

A great change already began to pass through my mind as to the one who was my travelling companion, and instead of feeling my own importance as a great and accomplished traveller, I felt more as a child compared with him. After tea, Mr. Chapman asked if I would like a walk, to which I readily assented, and we spent some time together in passing from one part of the city to another.

Presently, Mr. Chapman turned to me with the question, "Brother, do you know the way back to our hotel?"

"Know my way back! Why no, Mr. Chapman; I have never been in this city before."

"Very well, then, let us ask God to guide us."

Instantly, and before I had time to exclaim (which I did), I found myself drawn to the entrance of a side street, and heard Mr. Chapman in prayer, telling the Lord that we were in this city as His servants, and asking Him to guide us to the hotel, and to give us an opportunity of speaking to someone about his soul. I was dumb. I knew nothing about this intimate intercourse and spirit of constant dependence upon God, and I just followed on.

Presently, as we went down the street, Mr. Chapman, who had been scanning the names over the shops, stopped, and said, "That is an English name; let us go in." It was a bell hanger's, and, as we entered, a man in a paper cap came out from an inside room. Going towards him, and holding out his hand, Mr. Chapman said, "You are English?"

"Yes, that I am, and right glad I am to hear my mother tongue."

Mr. Chapman then said, "We are here to preach the Gospel," and asked the bell hanger if he was converted.

"This is the first time since I came into this country any one has asked me such a question, or cared anything about me. If that is your errand, you had better come inside."

I followed, wondering what would come of it. Mr. Chapman's Bible was out at once, and soon a most interesting conversation over the Scriptures was going on. The man was deeply in earnest, and prayer followed. Then, on rising from his knees, Mr. Chapman said, "We are strangers in the city; will you kindly direct us to ——— Hotel?"

"Direct you, sir; I'll go with you every step of the way," was the ready response, and he did so, while I was deeply impressed with the character of the man of God into whose presence and companionship I had so unexpectedly been brought.

The mission representative who related this incident said that when he returned to Seville years later, he sought out the bell hanger. As a result of his contact with Chapman, the bell hanger had become converted and was preaching the gospel.

The political turmoil in Spain made life dangerous for foreigners, who were often objects of suspicion. The Goulds and Lawrences began to suffer much opposition soon after they arrived and had to flee under great persecution only two years later. But with a determination born of the Lord, they returned several years after that. The Lawrences resumed their ministries in Barcelona and the Goulds ministered in Madrid.

After traveling and evangelizing in Spain and Portugal for about six months, Chapman returned to England. Encouraged by the opening vistas, in spite of the remaining dangers, he continued to preach on the spiritual needs in Spain. Religious liberty was proclaimed in Spain a few years later and a large number of British Christians were soon on their way there. These included Henry Payne and Albert Fenn. Payne was a Barnstaple Chapel convert and his wife was a teacher at the Bear Street Chapel day school. Fenn was teaching at a school in Bristol that was supported by George Müller. The two men and their wives traveled to Spain in October 1869; they started both day and night schools in Barcelona and cooperated with the Lawrences, who were also there.

But the country was still not safe for foreign missionaries. Albert Fenn narrowly escaped assassination during the second Carlist uprising in the early 1870s. After that, the Fenns moved to Madrid and worked with the Goulds, ministering God's Word until they died some twenty years later. Chapman corresponded constantly with all these courageous missionaries, offering encouragement and, as always, his prayers.

THE THIRD MISSIONARY TRIP

Chapman returned to Spain again in 1871. He was sixty-eight years old, the age when most men are ready to retire. But the evangelist had God's work to do. Although in excellent health, he did not walk across the country during this ten-month trip as he had done previously. He left England in April just after the Franco-German war ended. Traveling again through France, he found the French populace war-weary and discouraged. From Bordeaux he wrote in his poetic style: "The merry-hearted do sigh in this land, the look and voice of joy are no more....Many, alas, are only hardening their hearts under God's judgments, yet others have listened to us with reverence and thankfulness." He encountered many troops, both German and French, who were making their way back to their homes.

Chapman listened to their tales of horror in battle and of grief over the loss of comrades, and in turn he offered them the comfort and peace of Christ.

Crossing into Spain, Chapman came first to the town of San Sebastian, where an incident gave him reason to believe that he would see spiritual fruit in Spain. A government official told him that he had been led to Christ through Chapman's speaking to him some years previously! Chapman then traveled to Zaragosa, where a fair-sized Protestant church existed. Chapman sought out the pastor and they quickly became friends. "I write from Zaragosa," Chapman said, "a large city, among the chief in Spain for the worship of the Virgin; here is a Protestant preacher who listens to us with much love and reverence ...yet his understanding of the Gospel is small; his congregation, a large one, is almost wholly of the poor." Chapman preached daily for about two weeks in Zaragosa and during his last evening was invited to preach to a large crowd at the church of his new pastor-friend. He could not help but praise the Lord for the marked spiritual difference he could see, compared to his two earlier visits.

Chapman spent most of his time during this trip in Barcelona, where the Lawrences and Paynes and a good number of other missionaries worked. The Barcelona city administrators were more open to the work of foreign missionaries than officials elsewhere because the missionaries had mobilized an effective volunteer effort that had limited the extent of an epidemic that had threatened the city.

"We were met on our arrival," Chapman wrote, "by all our English brethren and some of the Spanish. On the Lord's Day morning we met in a school room for breaking bread." He rejoiced to see Spanish believers participating in active, simple worship. Of a blind man at the service, Chapman said, "The eyes of his heart had been opened by the Spirit of God....My heart is full of joy to see what God has wrought, and to see the good tokens of yet greater things." He was especially interested in the schools his missionary friends had established. After speaking to the children who were enrolled there, Chapman decided to visit some of their parents and was overjoyed to see that the Bibles given to the students were being used in the homes. The missionaries also arranged for Chapman to baptize several new converts after he arrived, a token of the fruit of his work. His letters back to England were filled with thanksgiving for what God had accomplished in Spain.

After several months in Barcelona, Chapman journeyed to Madrid, where he stayed with the Fenns and also with Mrs. Gould, whose husband had died recently. His work there was so satisfying that Chapman delayed his return to England. In August he wrote to the Christians at Barnstaple, "I am doing all diligence to return to you, yet am sure I ought to tarry in this land a while longer, and I judge somewhat longer than I expected when I left you." The Lord was blessing the work of His people and Chapman could not resist being a part of it. An incident in September showed the Lord's hand. Chapman wrote:

> Yesterday Brother Lawrence with his children and two Spanish brethren were in Barcelona purposing to distribute Gospels and other portions of Scripture among the crowd gathered [for] the King's entry into the town. One or two policemen bade him move from his place without any reason, but thus he was compelled to go into the midst of the procession of carriages and soldiers, and to follow in it not far from the King; all in [their] coach were occupied in giving out the Word of God; the soldiers even broke line to get the books.

As on his other missionary trips, Chapman seemed not to rest a moment. In October he wrote to the Bowdens, who were at home in Barnstaple in order to rest from their missionary work in India: "Last Monday Brother Fenn, Brother Lawrence, and myself visited Vilasar, a town on the mountains, where we lately began a school. At night we had about twenty five young men, to whom, after teaching them earthly things, each of us taking a class, we all spoke the Gospel."

Because Chapman had established contacts in Portugal during his previous visit, he wanted to visit them before returning to England. The opportunity arose in November, so a small group traveled first to Madrid by train. The ride was arduous, but the slow journey gave the Christians many opportunities to distribute Gospels whenever the train pulled into a station. At one station the railway inspector felt they were overstepping their bounds because the line and stations were private property. When policemen arrived to take the group before the mayor of the town, Chapman took the same stance that Jesus had often taken during His confrontations with the Pharisees and scribes. Taking money from his purse, he asked, "Have I a right to throw this to the poor who beg at the station? Here is bread; have I a right to give this also?" The officers, who could not answer, permitted the group to proceed.

As soon as they reached Madrid, the group bought train tickets to Lisbon, Portugal, and left on another train. When night came, they got off and found lodging. But those helping with their baggage told them—for they were obviously English and religious —that the landlord was a political zealot who possessed a violent temper. He had participated in the Carlist uprising the year before, so it would be dangerous, they cautioned, to engage him in a religious dialogue.

Chapman paid no heed to this advice, sought out the man, and said to him, "There is one thing which English and Spanish people need more than anything else."

"What is that?" asked the man.

"Peace with God. Have you that peace, my friend? I have had that peace through our Lord Jesus Christ for many years."

The others in the group were surprised at the man's mild reaction. He asked for some Gospels that he had seen them distribute and they quickly supplied him with all he wanted.

When they arrived in Lisbon, where Chapman had visited eight years before, he began a ten-day tour. He made a special point of seeking out a certain widow who for thirty years had run a school for the poor. She rejoiced to see Chapman again, "ever breaking forth in words of thanksgiving to God for sending us to her."

From Lisbon, Chapman wrote, "We have never once been rejected [here] in speaking of Christ and distributing the Scriptures." In December, he returned to Madrid to bid farewell to the missionaries there, then proceeded to Barcelona. After another month he bid his friends there good-bye. It is easy to sense his reluctance to leave; it was the last visit he would make to Spain.

Many years later Henry Payne wrote these words in tribute to his mentor:

> Mr. Chapman was a man of one book—the Bible....Not only was he a reader of the Bible, he also accompanied the reading with constant prayer....He watered with prayer the ground on which he trod. When [first] travelling in Spain, not knowing a single Christian in the whole country, he was not discouraged, but trusted in God. Years afterwards, when he saw the doors opened for the preaching of the Gospel...he was not in the least surprised; he had asked for it, and had patiently waited for the answer.

Chapman's trips to Spain and his constant prayers stimulated much missionary interest in that country and helped open it up to the gospel message. Consequently he could not help but praise God for the privilege of being His messenger: "Oh, to think of the pure Word of God being now freely spoken in any one corner of this dark land, which for 300 years has excluded the Scriptures and all the time been putting to death the children of God within its borders. Thanks be to God for His unspeakable gift!"

15
A Longtime Friend

Robert Chapman had many close friends and coworkers during his long life, but one stands out among them: William Hake. The two met in 1831—before Chapman moved to Barnstaple—at the home of the Thomas Pugsleys at Tawstock. As Müller and Craik had done a year earlier, Chapman and Hake at once found a natural bond, even though Hake was seven years older than Chapman and had a large family. Reminiscing on their friendship many years later, Chapman wrote: "Our hearts were presently knit together in the fellowship of the Spirit....Each found the other a lover of the Scriptures, and bent upon obedience to the Lord without reserve."

Unlike Müller and Craik, whose personalities were quite different, Chapman and Hake were quite similar. Each had a vivid manner of expressing himself and a good sense of humor. Hake's mother-in-law remembered William's reply when she told him, after he seceded from the Church of England, that he was cracked: "Yes, Mother;

the crack lets in the light." Just as Chapman was known for his wise sayings, so was Hake. One of Hake's proverbs goes, "When considering your faults and inclined to dejection concerning them, don't talk with yourself—don't keep bad company. Talk with the Lord."

Hake had needed to learn patience however. Born with a quick temper, he recognized its potential for hurting others and learned to conquer it. "My beloved fellow-laborer," wrote Chapman in a memorial to Hake, "was naturally so quick of nerves, that while of a tender, loving temperament, and full of consideration of others, he was soon angry; but God's grace is all sufficing to subdue what it forgives....He never failed of due self-judgment before God, and at length obtained such mastery over himself that few who knew him would suspect his natural infirmity."

Clearly Hake had a great influence on Chapman's thinking, as he had on so many others. Chapman often sought his advice and would travel to Exeter, forty miles to the south, to receive it. When Chapman decided to come to Barnstaple to continue his life's work, he wanted Hake to join him. But Hake felt it was not the will of God at that time since he was rearing a young family and had a worthwhile ministry as headmaster at a Christian boarding school. Disappointed, Chapman responded graciously, "I will not pluck the fruit until ripe and it falls into my lap."

Sometime during the 1840s Hake closed the boarding school and moved his family to Bideford, where he became the headmaster of a boarding school called Tusculum. This move delighted Chapman since Bideford was just ten miles west of Barnstaple and only about an hour away by carriage. From that time Chapman and the Hake family had frequent loving fellowship. Hake soon started a church meeting in his home in order to observe the Lord's Supper weekly. Initially the meeting consisted of just a few friends and family. They later rented a building and met in the manner of the other Assemblies.

Hake supervised Tusculum until 1860 when he became seriously ill and was given only a few months to live. A son, George, then took over his father's school responsibilities.

Amid many prayers for William's recovery, Elizabeth Hake took her sixty-five-year-old husband to Malvern, a popular spa. There a good friend, William Dyer, faithfully ministered to him and eventually Hake was restored to health.

USING THEIR HOME FOR GOD'S PURPOSES

In 1863 Chapman's good friend and helper, Bessie Paget, died at the age of eighty. Before her death she had arranged for the deed to her house at No. 9 New Buildings to be transferred to William and Elizabeth Hake. Shortly after they moved in (they lived at No. 9 for their remaining years), their unmarried daughter Elizabeth came to live with and care for them.

The Hakes, or perhaps the Assembly, added new rooms to the rear of the house. The new rooms included a large dining room. The Thursday evening meetings, which had long been held at No. 9, were expanded and moved to the new dining room. Even then not all the Christians from Bear Street Chapel who wanted to attend those meetings could fit in at the same time, and so they came on the Thursday evening designated for the district in which they resided. These popular district meetings consisted of the standard late-afternoon tea followed by what was called a Bible reading. Chapman and Hake both led this Bible reading and it became known for the fascinating dialogue that usually developed between the two friends. Guests at Chapman's frequently arranged to stay over until Friday so they could attend. A neighbor recalled that Chapman would take a long red carpet and lay it across the narrow dirt street from No. 6 to No. 9 just before Bible reading was to begin. The street was alternately dusty or muddy and the courteous Chapman wanted to provide the best for his guests.

Although not a gifted preacher, Hake was an excellent teacher and Chapman saw to it that this gift was used during the district meetings. Many of Hake's remarks during his teaching time were recorded. An example of his remarks is "Believe not your eyes if they contradict your

131

ears, provided it be God that speaks." During one Bible reading he stopped in the midst of John 15 and asked one of those present, "Would you like always to have your own way?" He then answered his own question by saying, "Well, I would. And this is how we can have it—'If ye abide in Me, and My words abide in you, ye shall ask what ye will, and it shall be done unto you.'" Possessing a beautiful bass voice, Hake loved to sing and was a regular participant in the weekly musical practices that were usually held at Chapman's house.

In addition to opening their home for meetings, the Hakes also used No. 9 as a home of rest for God's servants, just as Bessie Paget had done. The Hake and Chapman homes became "a resort for young disciples, where we, their elder brethren, have sought to cheer them on their way." H. B. Macartney, the Church of England clergyman quoted earlier in this book, recalled the first moments of his visit. Accompanied by other guests, he anxiously awaited Chapman's appearance and later wrote:

> At last Mr. Chapman entered, a strong-built man of about 70 with gray hair, beard, and moustache, the very image of Moses; and Mr. Hake followed, taller, but more bent, old and thin, and suffering. He reminded me of Aaron, the saint of the Lord. Such a kindly welcome from both the brothers, and then I listened to know how a man with such a reputation for holiness would converse—how he would differ from other men. A baby in a young mother's arms commenced to cry lustily, and I was rather annoyed at the interruption. Both Mr. Chapman and Mr. Hake spoke to the mother with the greatest concern and tenderness, and soon her baby slept. This was my first lesson there in the art of love.

Macartney stayed several days and wrote that Chapman "waited like a lover on Hake....The language of Canaan spread like a silver veil over the whole body of their conversation."

BELOVED BROTHER IN CHRIST

William Hake and Robert Chapman collaborated in ministering the Word of God. Called "the patriarchs" by the townspeople, they were a familiar sight as they walked the streets of Barnstaple together. Chapman usually held Hake's arm as they walked because the latter was no longer physically strong. They developed a systematic method of visitation throughout the town. Starting in the village of Newport on the southern edge of Barnstaple, they worked their way to Pilton on the north side, distributing gospel tracts and visiting whomever they could. Their lives and their loving concern for the townspeople were a great testimony to their Lord, who gave William Hake another twenty-five years of fruitful, happy service.

Chapman and Hake loved to play word games that dealt with the Scriptures. One would quote a brief portion of Scripture and challenge the other to finish it or place it in context. On one occasion they were walking some distance to speak at a school. The ground was covered with frost and after a while Hake remarked that it was good that neither had slipped. Chapman simply replied, "Remember Gideon." Hake knew this to be a challenge and reflected for some time on the connection to what Chapman had just said. It was a real puzzle because Gideon's life had been exemplary. Even after the Israelites offered to make him their king, he had refused saying, "The Lord shall rule over you" (Judges 8:23). But then Hake knew the answer. Gideon had next asked for the golden earrings taken from the Ishmaelites. From those he fashioned an ephod—an object used in divination—and "all Israel went thither a-whoring after it: which thing became a snare unto Gideon, and to his house" (8:27). After many years of service to God, Gideon had slipped.

There was never strife or bitterness between Chapman and Hake. "Ah, dear brother, we never had a jar," said Hake near the end of his life. Lovers of the Scripture, they were assured that God's Word was sufficient for them. Chapman related:

[We] daily contributed each to the other's treasure of grace and truth. In regard to the Scriptures that have been fulfilled, our unity of judgment was blessedly complete; as to what is yet to be fulfilled, we attained to an excellent measure of unity....We always waited on God together for His mind....If judgment did not agree, we waited on God to give us oneness of mind, and neither of us ever took a step against the judgment of the other—hence no strife, no bitterness!

This latter statement refers to the fact that Chapman and Hake did not agree on the interpretation of some prophecies. Chapman, for example, had taken a post-tribulational position for the rapture of the church, a position at variance with most of his friends. Although nonessential issues such as this frequently cause enmity between Christian friends, neither Chapman nor Hake permitted them to cause unhappiness between them. Their Christlike love overrode all disagreements.

A Peaceful Death at Age Ninety-Five

Mrs. Hake was not well and died in 1873. Another daughter, Mary Hake, took over her father's care when Elizabeth died in 1887. R. Fred Idenden, one of the Lord's servants who ministered in a nearby village and who later became one of the elders at Bear Street Chapel, also came over to Barnstaple during these years and helped Chapman and Hake with their work and correspondence.

In 1889 Chapman wrote to his friend Monsieur Dufour-Guisan of Lausanne, Switzerland, who had translated Chapman's *Choice Sayings* into French. Commenting on Hake, Chapman wrote, "He is now in his 95th year, but still enabled to continue in the service of Christ, in visiting from house to house, in reading the Scriptures (for which we have in his house a weekly meeting), also by the pen." In a letter written a few months later, Chapman referred to a now-weaker Hake as "the dear fellow-laborer with whom

I have walked in fellowship from December 1831." This date is neither the date of Chapman's first acquaintance with Hake in the summer of 1831 nor the date of Chapman's arrival in Barnstaple in April 1832. Perhaps it dates Chapman's first invitation to Hake to join him in the ministry at Ebenezer.

William Hake died at age ninety-five in 1890, active until the last. That same day he had walked with a visitor to the railway station. Later he came to the six o'clock tea at Chapman's home at which several people were present. He afterward sang with the group and for about an hour spoke on walking, standing, and sitting before God. Near the end of his talk, his speech failed, but he was able to walk with assistance to his bedroom. A few hours later he died, probably of a stroke.

The Hake family tombstone. *(photo courtesy of the author)*

Robert Chapman grieved greatly over his friend's death and could not bring himself to attend the funeral. But in a letter written at the end of 1890 he said, "Though so sorely bereaved, I am strengthened and guided to carry on the service in which I once had my loved yoke-fellow to bear burdens with me. 'The night is far spent, the day is at hand.'" This latter phrase, taken from Romans 13:12, frequently occurred in Chapman's letters during the last decade of his life.

Chapman soon began a memorial volume to his beloved friend entitled *Seventy Years of Pilgrimage*. The volume is principally a collection of some of Hake's letters and writings on the Scriptures, although both Chapman and Mary Hake wrote introductions. When we realize that Chapman had long ceased to publish any of his own writings, we clearly see the great value he placed on Hake's ministry.

After her father died, seventy-year-old Mary Hake took a special interest in the care of Chapman and even penned some of his letters. (She had known him since she was ten years old!) Not in good health, she died in October 1894, just four years after her father. Chapman wrote of her, "For myself I would say to loving friends, it has always been my desire to see her gone home first, and not to leave her behind me. God in granting me this desire has greatly comforted me. From her early days she has been as a daughter to me."

16
A Way with Words

Robert Chapman loved words. He loved to play with them, construct proverbs with them, and use them in unexpected ways. His ministry was much the richer for it. He loved English as much as the several other languages he mastered. The old schoolmaster William Hake said that he had not met anyone who knew the English language as well as Chapman; he could always choose the right words to express his thoughts. Reading Chapman now, we find his writings to be somewhat flowery and occasionally of unusual construction. We may attribute that to the style of a previous century, but Chapman's style was even a little out of the ordinary compared to that of his contemporaries. Hake called Chapman's language "classic English" because it was a combination of Anglo-Saxon and the words of Scripture.

SKILLED WITH PROVERBS

Chapman used proverbs in his teaching, not only because he personally enjoyed doing it, but also because he knew, as Jesus knew, that pithy sayings are easier to remember than straight prose. Many of his proverbs were recorded over a period of years by several friends who wanted to publish them, but Chapman resisted publication. In fact after the first decade or so of his ministry, he resisted the publication of any of his writings. This position was in striking contrast to the attitude of most of his friends in the Lord's work. Consider for example the voluminous output of such contemporaries as J. N. Darby and C. H. Spurgeon. Perhaps Chapman was afraid that for some people, his word could become a substitute for God's Word.

William Hake finally convinced Chapman to allow his proverbs to be published in a small volume entitled *Choice Sayings,* which has been reprinted many times. Spurgeon said of it, "The gold of that land is good." Chapman's hymns, of which 165 appeared in print, had been published many years earlier, as was his *Hymns and Meditations.* Fortunately some of his sermons and addresses are preserved in pamphlets such as *Goodly Words* and *The Good Shepherd.* Most of these pamphlets were published after his death.

ELOQUENT IN PREACHING

At John Street Chapel some of his peers told Chapman that he had no preaching gift. But he became an eloquent preacher. One of his favorite tasks was open-air preaching and until nearly the end of his life he preached regularly in Barnstaple in all kinds of weather. He usually preached in the town square or just across the road on the banks of the Taw river. Each year he also preached outdoors to the crowds attending the Barnstaple annual fairs. His powerful voice was no doubt very useful to him in open-air preaching. The obituary notice in the *North Devon Journal* (dated June 19, 1902) stated:

> A man of noble presence, Mr. Chapman was a most impressive preacher. His bell-like voice had great penetration power, so that when...he spoke in the open air his words could be distinctly heard by a very large assembly. His style was easy and natural. The uplifting of the hand to give emphasis was his characteristic gesture. But no pen could describe the power of his appeal.

One person characterized Chapman's voice as deep and rich; another said it was clear and melodious, as the evangelist Whitefield's voice is said to have been. Still others remarked on his skill in using inflections in his voice as he read or spoke. One who heard Chapman commend a lady for an act of Christian love wrote, "His manner and tone in which he said the words surpass description; it affected me greatly at the time."

USING SCRIPTURE TO TEACH

With notable exceptions—John Wesley comes to mind—the day-to-day activities of God's servants are usually not recorded. This was especially true of Chapman. The advice he gave and visits he made were not documented, and his counseling was confidential. But when stories were solicited for his memorials, it seemed that everybody had an anecdote to tell. Many of these anecdotes had to do with his teaching techniques.

When visiting the home of a believer who was having some sort of trial, one of Chapman's favorite methods of teaching was to quote a portion of Scripture and make a slight mistake. The believer would note the mistake, correct him, and then usually realize that a point was being made. "The Lord is my shepherd; I shall want," Chapman once read to a lady who was distressed about her future.

"I shall not want," she corrected him and then recognized her position and was ready to listen to Chapman's counsel.

Another time Chapman announced cheerfully to a new acquaintance, "I can do all things." The startled listener recovered quickly when Chapman added, "...through Christ which strengtheneth me" (Philippians 4:13).

When someone asked Chapman how he was feeling, or if at the end of a meal someone asked if he had had enough to eat, one of his favorite replies was simply "Satisfied and full." If the inquirer didn't know what was coming next, he soon learned, for Chapman would merrily add, "Satisfied with favour, and full with the blessing of the Lord" (Deuteronomy 33:23).

Once when a person asked, "How are you?" Chapman said that he was burdened. The concerned inquirer was much relieved to hear him continue, "He daily loadeth us with benefits" (see Psalm 68:19).

John Knox McEwen, a pioneering evangelist in Nova Scotia, related the following story. Chapman and Hake had invited him to come to their home of rest. On the first day of his visit, McEwen was talking with Chapman while Hake was absent. During a pause in the conversation Chapman said, "Mr. Hake is a very provoking brother. He has been provoking me all morning." McEwen was quite startled to hear this remark coming from a man whose kindness was well known. But his surprise did not last long, for Chapman continued, "Mr. Hake has been provoking me all morning to love and good works" (see Hebrews 10:24).

In order to urge acquaintances to memorize Bible verses so they would be readily accessible for meditation or use in conversation, Chapman often quoted the first part of a verse and waited for the one addressed to complete it. This approach could be quite threatening to a person unable to give the answer, but Chapman seems always to have done this with such sensitivity that people were not offended. A guest who stayed at Chapman's house when Chapman was ninety-eight years old heard the following exchange with another visitor: "Let patience have her————." The answer was given after some hesitation, so Chapman repeated it with emphasis: "...perfect work, that ye may be perfect and entire, wanting nothing." Then he added a few words to help fix James 1:4 in mind. This visitor later said, "I used to think, as I sat listening, that I would much rather hearken to Mr. Robert Chapman expounding God's Word than the most gifted Hebrew and Greek Doctor of Divinity that could be found."

Chapman's acquaintances among scholars and preachers often remarked on his profound knowledge of the Scriptures and his unusual grasp of their deeper meaning. But he denied the suggestions of some that he had recovered truths the church had long forgotten. "I know of no recovered truths," he replied. "I hold nothing that others have not held before me." He would not claim a new revelation as some others have—both in his time and today.

More than once after a morning walk Chapman returned home and announced, "I have had a large congregation this morning." On inquiry it would be discovered that he had spoken to but a single person. A receptive heart is indeed a large congregation!

THE IMPORTANT ROLE OF BOOKS

Books had a formative influence on the young Chapman. As we have seen, Italian literature particularly fascinated him. More than one person remarked on his extensive knowledge of it. His translation of the poem of Michelangelo, quoted earlier in this book, illustrates the attraction that Italian literature continued to have for him. Thus it is a little surprising to read in several Chapman memorials that he regularly advised his audiences to confine their reading to the Bible.

His admonitions probably had as much to do with religious literature as with secular. Not much good Christian literature was available in Chapman's day and some of what passed for Christian literature was not biblically founded. A new believer usually has difficulty discerning whether a religious article is soundly based, but the Bible is God's sure Word. "Men's books full oft with chaff are stored, God's naught but golden grain afford," Chapman liked to say. This couplet suggests that Chapman's attitude was cautionary rather than prohibitive, as one of his existing letters also attests.

Still the mature Chapman's preferred reading was in the Bible. He did not occupy himself much with daily newspapers. One day a newsboy asked him to buy a newspaper. Chapman asked, "Does it give yesterday's news?"

"Oh no, sir!" the boy replied.

"Has it today's news?"

"Yes sir!"

"And has it tomorrow's news?" Chapman held up his Bible to the surprised boy and said, "This book gives me the news of yesterday, today, and tomorrow as well!"

Someone once asked Chapman if he had read a certain new book. Chapman laid his hand on his Bible and lovingly replied, "I have not finished this yet."

STORYTELLING AT ITS BEST

Not surprisingly, Chapman became a good storyteller. He loved to tell anecdotes and construct allegories, which he always directed toward spiritual lessons. One of his allegories may be connected with his period of trial when potential guests did not respond to his invitation to share his hospitality at his rest home. He had been teaching from Ephesians 5 on giving thanks always to God. A listener remarked that she could not always do that, and Chapman replied, "There must be some cause; you must have some little business of your own in a corner." Chapman knew that when a Christian has kept God out of a certain portion of his life, he has "some little business of his own in a corner" and will be unable to give thanks for lessons learned when an apparently adverse event occurs. After replying in this way, Chapman realized that he should apply this lesson to himself. A little later he constructed this allegory in his classic English:

The Partners Three [an allusion to the trinity] beheld me sitting in my rags and filth, and in a great concern pitied me, took me up, washed me, clothed me, and took me into partnership. Such was the wisdom, power, and skill of the Partners that everything prospered. Everything went on well and music flowed from the harp in my hand. But in an evil hour it came into my head to set up a little business of my own in a corner. I set up my little wheels and had a brass plate put on the door with this inscription: "All manner of earthenware and brittle goods repaired here by Messrs. Self-will, Self-wisdom, & Co." During all this time my harp was hung on the willows, and I could not sing; everything was going wrong with me. I could get nothing but vexation and disappointment. Remember now, my back was turned all this time against the great business, but the Partners Three in a great concern saw me, pitied me, and then caused the great wheel of their business to roll over mine and put it all in ruins. I beheld, considered, and turned to the Partners Three, made a full confession, and was received back without upbraiding; and my harp that had been hung on the willows was taken in my hand again. Ah! but it yields a music now more deep and more solemn than heretofore.

We can infer from this allegory that Chapman must have had an experience in his Christian life when he undertook something in self-will and did not bring God into the picture. His project failed and he learned a valuable lesson.

17
Apostle of Love

Chapman knew that one who is called to give himself entirely to the Lord's work holds a special place of responsibility. This is how he put it:

> The servant of the Lord Jesus must be instant in season and out of season, knowing that he is the Lord's messenger to every one with whom he has to do, and ever learning of the Lord; seeing that he is to be continually ministering to others, he must be receiving fresh supplies from the God of all grace through all channels. Meditation on the Word and prayer should occupy the chief part of his time. In his public ministry and in his private conversation he should aim at hearts and consciences, seeking in every way to magnify Christ and abase the creature. In short, he should set the Lord always before him, and so walk in His steps as to represent Him to every eye.

From Chapman's great devotion to Christ and his commitment to magnify Him sprang a deep love and care for people. A hymn of his contains the following verse, and those who knew him said it well expressed his attitude:

> Thy brethren, Lord, are my delight,
> I love them strong or weak;
> They all are precious in my sight,
> The froward with the meek.

The froward or contrary brethren are always around, but Chapman learned how to deal with them through his spirit of love. With this attitude of heart, Chapman was a true shepherd and counselor of the flock at Bear Street Chapel. People often came to him for advice in family matters even though he never married. He helped many husbands and wives regain their respect and love for one another through a proper understanding of what the Bible says about the marriage relationship. When he was with just one spouse, he would keep the attention focused on that person, not the absent one; he wanted that person to recognize his or her faults first. He stressed the importance of a right relationship with God as the proper beginning for a right relationship with another person. This, he believed, was to be accomplished through prayer and repentance. Chapman was also firmly against the marriage of a believer to an unbeliever.

Because of Chapman's reputation for godly wisdom and love for all people, he was frequently called on to deal with difficulties that churches experience. He did this so often that people recognized a pattern: he would usually begin by convening a meeting of the whole church and at that meeting he would preach on the high responsibility of the church on earth; after that he would consider the specific details of the problem.

His patience was notable, but his human side sometimes showed itself. After a difficult Christian man came to live in Barnstaple, someone asked Chapman how things were going with that brother. He replied, "We did not know our need of patience till he came among us."

Robert Chapman carefully observed people, a skill that helped him deal with tough situations. A lady on whom he called one day would not invite him in, but began berating him on the doorstep for some perceived wrong. Chapman turned to a brother who was waiting nearby and said, "Dear brother, listen to this dear sister; she is telling me all that is in her heart." She was then unable to continue. When someone would come to Chapman with a story about the misconduct of someone else, he typically asked the complainer to go with him to confront the person directly, believing that both sides must be heard before any judgment could be made.

Of course not everyone liked Chapman. Some people were greatly offended by his plain preaching on sin and the need for repentance. A touching story is told of his love and concern for one of those critics. A grocer in Barnstaple became so upset when Chapman was preaching in the open air that he strode up to where Chapman was standing and spit on him. Later one of Robert's wealthy relatives came to Barnstaple to visit him and to try to understand his activities. Arriving by horse-drawn cab at the address given to him, the relative at first would not believe that Chapman lived in such a simple abode in such a poor neighborhood. Chapman ushered him into the clean but simple interior and explained what living in dependence on the Lord meant and how the Lord had provided for all his needs. The relative asked if he could purchase groceries for him. Chapman gladly assented, but stipulated that he must buy the food from a certain grocer. The relative went there, made a large purchase, and paid the bill. When the grocer learned that the food was to be delivered to R. C. Chapman, he said that the visitor must have come to the wrong shop. Chapman's relative, however, replied that Chapman himself had specifically directed him to that shop. The grocer, who had viciously attacked and castigated Chapman for years, broke down in tears. Soon he came to Chapman's house, asked forgiveness, and yielded his life to Christ.

An incident that occurred before Chapman came to

Barnstaple was a great object lesson to him about faithfulness in prayer:

> When I knew Bond Street, London, seventy years ago, it was the principal resort for worldly men. Well, there lived a shoemaker there, a very spiritual and godly man; and regularly each day he would retire from his business at twelve o'clock to pray for an hour, and he would tell his assistants and apprentices by no means to call or disturb him.
>
> One day an earl called and requested to see the shoemaker, but the assistant remarked, "He is engaged, and is never to be called at that hour."
>
> "Not to be called!" said the earl, impatiently; "not to be called!" he repeated, and he left the shop angrily.
>
> The assistant concluded that he would never see him again; but one day, to the astonishment of all, he called at the shop, and requested to see the shoemaker. He had been going to other shops in the meantime, but he had failed to get fit and satisfaction.

So the earl returned to the faithful shoemaker, and many times thereafter, never calling on him during his appointed hour for prayer.

Chapman's intimate familiarity with the Scriptures and his constant prayers, spoken in the knowledge that his Father heard him, affected all aspects of his life. His delight in prayer overflowed into his hymns, such as this one that begins:

> O how I love in solitude,
> Great God, to speak with Thee,
> For Thou whose grace my soul renewed,
> A Father art to me.

He regarded intercessory prayer as a special ministry. He said, "It is well for a child of God to pray for himself, but a more excellent thing to pray for others." His list of those to pray for was practically endless; he would pray for them by name. One day a lady he knew asked him to remember her children in prayer. He replied gravely, "I cannot begin to pray for your dear children." Startled, she began to apologize for imposing, but Chapman quickly interrupted her, stating cheerfully that he could not begin because he had already begun.

As we have seen, when Robert Chapman was first converted many of his family rejected him. Rather than just accepting this rejection as the inevitable consequence of turning to the Lord in faith, Chapman prayed regularly for them and did his best to keep communication open. He did not give up on them and later saw the spiritual fruit of his effort when several of his brothers and sisters were converted. Truly "the effectual fervent prayer of a righteous man availeth much" (James 5:16).

CHAPMAN'S DEEP LOVE FOR CHILDREN

Although he had no children of his own, Chapman was very conscious of children and as concerned for them as for anyone. "Ask not merely for their conversion," he would advise parents, "but that they may be well-pleasing children of God and servants of Christ." In one of his last sermons, which was directed toward the training of children by their parents, he said, "There are so many people who are satisfied with just knowing they are saved. Tell them not to be satisfied with this. I want them to study the Word, and grow in the knowledge of God. Tell them I want them to become intimate with the Lord Jesus Christ."

Several people recalled his common question to parents regarding a child: "Does he obey at the first word?" As most parents know, the answer to this question is usually no. The matter is often a constant source of friction between parent and child as the child grows older and strives to assert his or her independence. Parents to whom this question was addressed could well dismiss it as characteristic of an unmarried man who had no children of his own, but those who remembered his emphasis on obedience accepted it as valuable advice from a beloved friend and teacher.

Chapman was not at all awkward around children. He loved them, paid special attention to them when he visited their homes, and seems to have had a special kinship with them. H. B. Macartney said, "Communion with God makes him childlike." About 1890, when he was in his eighties, Chapman visited Scotland and was a guest at the house of J. R. Caldwell. Caldwell observed:

> He was mentally and physically fresh and vigorous. He rose early as was his wont, yet was able to address meetings nearly every evening, and his ministry was such as to leave a lasting impression upon all who heard....Mr. Chapman chiefly emphasized the reading of and meditation upon the whole of the Scriptures....A bright, genial, loving and attractive spirit drew out the confidence even of the little ones. He used to play with our little girl, then two or three years old, in the afternoons at a childish game on the carpet, just as if he were a child again himself; and one morning before the household was awake, he had made a paper kite for our son, then about six years old, and was out with him by nine o'clock helping him to fly it. Truly the memory of his visit remains with us as a precious illustration of how far God can reproduce in a believer even here the image of His Son.

A lady recounted that when she was a young girl, Chapman asked her, "Can you tell me, my dear, why Jesus was led as a lamb to the slaughter?" She had not thought of that before. Chapman did not give her the answer but left her with the question. She later asked her mother about it and was directed to Isaiah 53. There she read, "But he was wounded for our transgressions, he was bruised for our iniquities: the chastisement of our peace was upon him; and with his stripes we are healed. All we like sheep have gone astray; we have turned every one to his own way; and the Lord hath laid on him the iniquity of us all."

Then she understood the question as well as the answer, and opened her heart to her Savior.

Chapman's friend, H. W. Soltau, recounted how his children loved to have Chapman visit them because *they* liked to talk to *him.* On one occasion Chapman and others were guests at a meal and several children were present. Chapman was seated first, then surprised everyone by insisting that the children be seated with him instead of at their separate table. The other adults and the hostess bore with him in good humor and the children were delighted to use the grown-ups' dishes and sit at the grown-ups' table.

SENSITIVITY TO OTHERS' NEEDS

Being sensitive to other people's needs is not always easy, but Chapman was both sensitive and thoughtful. An example of his thoughtfulness was his habit of beginning and ending meetings on time; he knew that many in attendance were servants who were expected to be back at a certain hour.

Annual conferences, popular among the Assemblies, were convened throughout Britain to provide encouragement and a forum for discussion of doctrine and practice. Chapman instituted an annual conference at Barnstaple some years after Bear Street Chapel was started. He invited speakers from throughout Britain, but refused to schedule the talks to accommodate only the speakers; he also took into consideration the local train timetable so that his people could get to the railroad station in time to catch their rides back home.

His thoughtfulness extended even to his handwriting. As he grew older, his handwriting became more difficult to read. One day William Hake had to mention that he could not read a note Chapman had given him. Chapman then determined not to impose this hardship on recipients of his correspondence. Through deliberate attention, he markedly improved his penmanship from that time on. He was the type of leader God wants: a servant-leader who puts the needs of others first.

This autograph by Chapman was written after he was 99.

CERTAIN OF GOD'S PROVISION

Chapman did not consider his faith to be other than what should be expected of a Christian. His sermons and conversations were sprinkled with exhortations to live by faith. To him, thanksgiving was a natural consequence of such faith. "Do you count up your mercies?" he would ask. "Do your thanksgivings keep pace with them?" A great object of Chapman's public and private ministry was to encourage and strengthen faith, and he lived in the sure faith that God would supply all his needs.

William Hake told the following story: He and Chapman were visiting in South Devon and as usual had just enough money for two railway fares back to Barnstaple. Since they needed to separate, Hake gave Chapman the money for his return fare. Later they met again and Hake, knowing Chapman's habits, asked him if he had his fare. Chapman answered, "Our Father knows all about it." Hake suspected what had happened and as they approached the station asked him again. Chapman confessed that he had given the money to an elderly lady who was not feeling well and needed the money.

"Well, what are you going to do now?" Hake asked.

"Our Father knows all about it," Chapman said again.

They arrived at the station and waited for the train, Hake being greatly agitated. As the train drew up to the platform, a friend of theirs hurried up, apologized for being late, and handed them each a sum of money that more than covered their fares.

152

Mr. George Fisher, who helped Chapman in his later years and accompanied him when traveling, related a similar story. They were ready to leave a conference at Leominster, but neither had any money. Chapman had been given some at the conference, but had almost immediately given it to someone who he felt needed it more. On the way to the railway station Fisher reminded Chapman that they had no money. Mr. Chapman replied, "To whom does the money belong, and the cattle upon a thousand hills?"

When they reached the station, a man on an arriving train recognized Chapman, hurried over, handed him a five-pound note, and said, "I have had this in my pocket for some time, and am glad I met you." He then got back on his train, which departed. After a moment Chapman asked his companion, "To whom does the money belong?"

James Mansfield related that he once came to the railway station in Barnstaple and saw Chapman sitting in a car on the waiting train. Mansfield struck up a conversation and after a few moments, suspecting the situation, asked Chapman to show him his purse. This Chapman did with a smile. It contained no money and no ticket. Chapman had come to the station confident that the Lord would provide a ticket if it was His will that he undertake the journey. Mansfield supplied his needs, knowing he was the Lord's agent that day.

Chapman delighted in attending various annual conferences. He was a frequent speaker and greatly enjoyed the company of his fellow laborers. One day at a Leominster conference he seemed to be burdened. Later however he was his usual cheerful self. His friends learned afterward that he had been given a considerable sum of money, which weighed him down until he distributed it among several people.

A FEW RECOLLECTIONS

Even people who had little use for the truths of God would refer to Chapman, usually not in derision, as a man of God or "that holy man." Many people believed that God specially protected him. Once when he boarded a coach, the coachman announced to the other riders in good humor, "You need not insure your lives today, gentlemen; Mr. Chapman is going with us."

A similar incident occurred on the newly constructed rail line from Exeter to Barnstaple in the mid-1850s. As the train descended the steep hill leading to Barnstaple, a lady became terrified. She was comforted by the coachman, who assured her that there was no danger because Mr. Chapman was on the train.

Telling his visitor that all Protestants must be lost because they were outside the true church, a local Roman Catholic paused, reflected, and added, "Well, there is one in Barnstaple who will get to heaven if anyone will....I don't know his name, but he lives on New Buildings Street. He is the oldest and holiest man in Barnstaple."

An elderly woman who was a native of Barnstaple told Charles Fraser-Smith that while she and her brother worked at Chapman's houses during the 1880s, Winston Churchill, then a young boy, had been brought to visit Chapman.

As a young woman, one of Fraser-Smith's aunts felt a call to go to Spain to work among the children at what was then the Children's Special Service Mission. Knowing of Chapman's long-standing influence among missionaries to Spain and his wise counsel, she took the train to Barnstaple to seek his advice. The elderly Chapman heard her aspirations and asked her to come back the next morning before her departure. The next morning he gave her his approval and blessing and prayed with her for her safety in the new work. During the prayer the cab arrived to take her to the station; she heard it come but didn't want to break into Chapman's lengthy prayer. The cab waited, but they arrived at the station after the train had left. A few hours later she learned that the train had been involved in a serious accident. She took this incident as confirmation of the Lord's provision for her safety and went on to Spain.

A soldier who had lived in Barnstable recounted this

story to missionary F. S. Arnot: Upon returning home at dawn after his all-night sprees, the soldier would frequently meet an old man walking with Bible in hand. The old man would stop the soldier and talk to him about his sins. Years later the memory of these interactions with Chapman was instrumental in the soldier's conversion to Christ.

Chapman often preached on controlling the tongue. After one such sermon, a young woman who had separated from her husband and had rejected Chapman's attempts at counseling admonished him for exposing her in public. Chapman assured her that he did not have her in mind as he prepared the sermon, but that the Holy Spirit was surely speaking to her heart. She accepted this and not long afterward was reunited happily with her husband.

Thus the years passed for Robert Chapman—years of giving, years of peace, years of love. Some Christian leaders gain fame as orators, evangelists, organizers, or theologians. But few achieve lasting fame as apostles of love. This is what Chapman achieved because of his determination to *live* Christ.

18
Friends and Acquaintances

Caring, loving people usually have many friends and this was the case with Robert Chapman. His spirit is caught in this remembrance of a visitor to his home: "I can hear his loving voice even now exclaiming, 'I'm delighted to see you, yes, delighted to see you. Welcome, my dear brother!'"

His friends were not just those of a small coterie; they included both poor and rich, unknown and well-known. His acquaintances were from all strata of society. For example Chapman corresponded with W. E. Gladstone, thrice prime minister of England. He also knew Samuel Wilberforce, a prominent Anglican clergymen whose politician father had fought the slave trade; the elder Wilberforce's fight against slavery in the British empire led to emancipation in 1833. Our story has already mentioned several of Chapman's friends and acquaintances, but many more deserve a brief mention.

CHARLES HADDON SPURGEON

Charles Haddon Spurgeon was the dynamic, spell-binding Baptist preacher whose home base was the large Metropolitan Tabernacle in London. His public ministry was vastly different from Chapman's, yet the two men were alike in many ways. Their devotion to God and the authority of the Bible was the highest; they were both willing to break new ground; and they were both ardent evangelists. Although Spurgeon was a Particular Baptist—a denomination with which Chapman would not affiliate—neither man let that be a barrier to their friendship or communication. Spurgeon called Chapman the saintliest man he ever knew, and greatly valued Chapman's book *Choice Sayings*.

Toward the end of his relatively brief life of fifty-eight years, Spurgeon became isolated from many Baptist leaders because of his outspoken stand against the growing popularity of so-called higher criticism. Chapman had passed through the agony of division within the Brethren movement and could well sympathize with Spurgeon's anguish. Always the comforter, Chapman visited Spurgeon at his London home and was there again a short time before Spurgeon died.

J. HUDSON TAYLOR

In 1852 when the twenty-year-old J. Hudson Taylor, who was burdened for China, learned about the wisdom and missionary concern of Robert Chapman, he eagerly sought Chapman's advice. After Taylor established his initial work in China, his rather autocratic style and insistence that English missionaries eat and dress like the Chinese created much opposition from many supporters in England. Returning to England, he met again with Chapman in 1863 in the London home of George Pearse of the Chinese Evangelization Society. Taylor was then thinking of establishing an interdenominational mission organization to be called the China Inland Mission. Chapman encouraged him and became one of CIM's first "referees"—supporters and advisers who answered inquiries about the mission. Chapman's friend George Müller, through his Scriptural Knowledge Institution, also became a substantial financial supporter of CIM, which was underway by 1866.

Taylor visited Chapman several times in Barnstaple. An undated letter from Barnstaple reads in Chapman's characteristic style: "My dear brother Taylor, Consider our claim on you. We desire fellowship with you in your work. Oh! come and speak to us your brethren here. Say when you can come....God delights to fill our open mouths." When they met again in 1872, Chapman's affectionate greeting was noted: "I have visited you every day since you went to China!" He had prayed for Taylor daily by name.

HENRY W. SOLTAU

Henry W. Soltau, prominent in the large Assembly in Plymouth during its early days, had been born into a wealthy merchant family, as had Chapman. Like Chapman, Soltau had also become a lawyer. The Soltau family had long been staunch Anglicans, but Henry was converted in 1837 after hearing a sermon by Percy Hall. He then abandoned the legal profession (but not his wealth) to evangelize the small villages and hamlets around Plymouth. Later he opened a store for the distribution of Christian literature. He met Chapman during his years at Plymouth and the two became good friends.

Soltau, who could not agree with J. N. Darby's decision in 1845 to set up a new Assembly in Plymouth, stayed loyal to B. W. Newton until shortly before Newton's departure from Plymouth at the end of 1847. Feeling that his position among the Brethren at Plymouth was hopelessly compromised because of his support of Newton, Soltau moved his family to Exmouth in 1848. When William Hake, then headmaster at the school in Bideford, offered him a teaching position, Soltau gladly accepted. In 1851 he moved his family to Bideford, close to his friends Chapman and Hake. There he could live in a more cloistered environment and continue to write on his favorite Old Testament themes and teach.

Mrs. Soltau had never been baptized as a believer because the Plymouth Assembly had not stressed baptism. But after the Soltaus moved to Bideford and came under the strong influence of Hake and Chapman, she and her daughters saw the importance of it. In 1854 Robert Chapman baptized her and her three daughters in the river that ran through Bideford.

During these years the Soltaus became aware of Hudson Taylor's work, probably through Chapman. Following Müller's example, they also supported Taylor's work. True to his belief in the unity of all Christians, Soltau gave his blessing to his son Henry when he joined China Inland Mission as a medical missionary and to his daughter Henrietta when she began her lifelong work at the CIM headquarters in England.

When Soltau's health began to fail, he moved to Barnstaple in 1870 to be closer to his good friends, for Hake had relocated there. Soltau died in 1875 and his son was the principal speaker at Chapman's funeral some twenty-seven years later. In this sermon the younger Soltau said that with Chapman gone, the Christians would have to lean more on Christ; this interesting remark gives substance to Chapman's reluctance to publish or otherwise promote himself.

MR. AND MRS. SWAINE BOURNE

Mr. and Mrs. Swaine Bourne of Birmingham often hosted Chapman when he visited the midlands of England. Mrs. Bourne, who had lived in Barnstaple as a girl, was the daughter of a prominent member of the Church of England. She had attended Bear Street Chapel and had been converted through Chapman's ministry. Wanting to be baptized, she informed her father of her desire, but he became quite angry and refused to give her permission. When she persisted, he told her she would not be welcome in his home if she went through with the baptism. Still convinced that she must obey the Lord's request, she was baptized by Chapman in the Taw river. Upon arriving home, she was welcomed by her father and knew that she had the Lord's blessing. The Swaine Bournes remained close friends of Chapman until his death.

W. H. BENNET AND E. H. BENNETT

W. H. Bennet's career as a servant of the Lord began with Robert Gribble, with whom he worked for a short while before Gribble's death. Bennet knew Chapman well during Chapman's later years and wrote a long memorial biography that was published a few months after Chapman's death. E. H. Bennett of Cardiff, Wales, knew Chapman for forty years and wrote a shorter memorial to him that contains this interesting statement concerning Chapman's work in Spain: "Chapman and others were tried and sentenced in absence in Spain for circulating God's Word."

DENHAM SMITH

Denham Smith, a well-known evangelist, also became a good friend of Chapman. Smith's work centered around Dublin after the religious revival that swept the British Isles in 1859. Smith once told Chapman that someone should write his biography. Chapman replied, "It is being written, and will be published in the morning." Expressing his views on biographies on another occasion, Chapman said, "If you want the perfect model biography, you may find it in Genesis 5:21-24 and Hebrews 11:5." Who was this perfect model? Enoch, who walked with God.

JAMES WRIGHT

James Wright, who became the director of George Müller's Ashley Downs orphanages when Müller was old, was a longtime friend of Chapman. Wright recorded his first meeting with Chapman in 1841. Chapman had spoken at a Sunday school meeting in another part of the city in the afternoon and came to Bethesda Chapel in the evening. Wright especially remembered Chapman's marvelous voice and how his simple delivery and inflection of voice rendered a great sympathy for the gospel message. He recalled someone saying, "To hear Mr. Chapman only read a psalm is as good as a sermon." Wright continued:

> Doubtless the flexibility and skillful inflections of his voice had something to do with it; still more, his unusual grasp of the deeper meanings of Holy Scripture. But...I believe the true explanation is to be found in the intense reverence for and love of the God-breathed words....One result of his listening so intently to the voice of God was that Mr. Chapman excelled in the habit of speaking to God in prayer.

The former Müller orphanage at Ashley Downs.
(photo courtesy of the author)

When Wright asked G. F. Bergin to become the associate director of the orphanages, Bergin at once went to Barnstaple and laid the proposal before Robert Chapman. Reassured of his fitness for the task, Bergin accepted. After Chapman died in 1902, Bergin wrote:

> [He] was one of George Müller's oldest and most intimate friends. More than once, in critical periods of this work, Mr. Müller sought and obtained his valuable counsel. This confidence Mr. Chapman responded to by always showing the liveliest interest in the progress of the Institution. Throughout the 68 years of its existence he has been its helper by continuous intercession. It was the knowledge that he was such a mighty spiritual helper that led me, in the spring of 1901, to visit Barnstaple....It was no small confirmation to learn...from his own lips that he most heartily and unreservedly approved of our modifying the conditions [in the management of the orphanage].

HENRY GROVES

Henry Groves, a son of Anthony Norris Groves, very much shared the "open" sentiments of his father and in the latter half of the nineteenth century became a recognized leader among the open Brethren. He was the first editor of *Echoes of Service*, a missionary magazine that started in 1872, and he coaxed articles from Chapman on missionary work in Spain and elsewhere. As already mentioned, Chapman did not like to see his name in print, feeling that it drew unwarranted attention to himself. Nevertheless he saw the need and contributed several articles to the magazine.

A few of Chapman's other writings also made it into print. *Truth in Season,* for example, is a collection of essays by W. J. Stokes, Henry Dyer, and Chapman. Henry Dyer was the brother of William Dyer, who nursed Hake back to health after his serious illness in 1860. Henry and Chapman did not agree on some matters of prophecy, but they did not let that interfere with their close fellowship, as we will see in a later chapter.

19
Doctrines Essential and Nonessential

Chapman received no formal theological training, but that was not unusual in his day. Many clergymen of the Church of England received almost none. He had learned at the feet of Harington Evans and must have studied many writings of the great reformers. Although he developed much of his Scriptural understanding during interaction with his friends, Chapman's theology was Bible-derived.

A THEOLOGY BASED ON THE BIBLE

Chapman's doctrinal positions were formed on one premise: the whole Bible must be studied. "Our hearts were assured of the fulness of the Word of God....While colour can be found in it for well-nigh any false doctrine ...no error can abide the test of the whole Scripture."

These sentences from Chapman's memorial to William Hake are typical of his repeated emphasis that one must not develop a theological position based on only a fragment of the Scriptures, removed from its context. A thorough student of the Word, Chapman took care that his preaching was balanced. His thoughts on the Bible are well expressed in some of his meditations:

> The Book of God is a store of manna for God's pilgrim children....The great cause of neglecting the Scriptures is not want of time, but want of heart, some idol taking the place of Christ....A child of God who neglects the Scriptures cannot make it his business to please the Lord of Glory....If the Bible be used aright by anyone, it will be to him the most pleasant book in the world....It is one thing to read the Bible, choosing something that suits me (as is shamefully said), and another thing to search it that I may become acquainted with God in Christ. [If I do the former] I turn the Gospel of Christ into the law of Moses without knowing it, and, instead of paths of pleasantness and peace, the Gospel of Christ becomes bands of iron.

The last sentence, among many others, shows that Chapman distinguished between God's commandments to the children of Israel and God's grace given to the church.

Although Chapman is remembered for his gentle and forgiving spirit, he occasionally used biting wit to emphasize specific points, such as his objection to higher criticism. About 1860 higher criticism of the Bible was attracting adherents in Britain, and C. H. Spurgeon had run into much opposition when he preached strongly against it. (Higher criticism is the philosophy that starts from the following assumptions: the Bible is not the inspired Word of God, but a collection of stories designed to illustrate certain truths; many Biblical characters never existed; and many events described in the Bible never happened.)

After a meal during which the subject of higher criticism arose, Chapman constructed this allegory:

> One day, while walking in the noon-day light of a mid-summer sun, beneath a cloudless sky, I was accosted by a person wholly a stranger to me, who, with kind, condescending air, made offer to show me the way. I saw in his hand a lantern, and in it a lighted [penny] candle. Pity checked my rising laughter; so, as gravely as I could, I declined his offer, and went on my way. I was afterwards told that his name was Higher Criticism.

Chapman did not trust anyone else's writings until he proved their consistency with the Bible. His admonitions to people to make the Bible their focus of reading probably reflected this aspect of his personality. There is also a very human tendency, even in Christian circles, to dwell on and argue over people's writings, sometimes to the near exclusion of reading God's Word. Doubtlessly this is the primary reason why Chapman published very little.

He generally viewed the Scriptures from the dispensationalist perspective, although he did not emphasize it as some others did. For example, instead of dwelling on the dispensational distinctions between God-fearing peoples who lived during different times, he emphasized their oneness, as in the following: "All in Adam die through Adam, and all in Christ have life in Him. This must be common to the elect of God of every age, every one [of the elect] being created anew. All have life derived from the Son of God, whether before or after He had come in the flesh."

Before espousing a position on controversial interpretations, he would study a matter for many years. B. W. Newton complained that Chapman had no clear notion of the prophesied millennial period to come at the endtimes, and this may be true for the period that Newton knew him. Chapman said once that when he came to a "settled judgment" on a particular Scripture, he never found reason to alter that judgment. Sometimes this led him to take a position at variance with his peers.

CHAPMAN'S PERSPECTIVE ON IMPORTANT ISSUES

Baptism and Christian Unity

Baptism, Calvary, and the unity of all believers were important concepts to Chapman, who often preached on these subjects. He gave baptism a high priority in the experience of a new believer and baptized people in the Taw river until he was eighty. He taught that baptism by immersion expressed the believer's identification with the burial and resurrection of Christ. However he strongly opposed the teaching that baptism has any saving influence. After his early period at Ebenezer, he did not permit baptism to be a condition of membership there or later at Bear Street Chapel, nor did he allow it to be a prerequisite for participation in the Lord's Supper. At age ninety-five he wrote in a letter:

> The baptism of the Lord...set forth in simplest fashion His own death, and burial, and resurrection, and that of all His members. When by the Word and Spirit of God a child of Adam is [brought] from death to life, that child of God is a member of the body whereof Christ is the Head, and all the obligations of the new covenant bind the members to each other. If the newly-born be ignorant or neglectful touching the precious figure, water baptism, such ignorance or neglect must be rightly dealt with. But how? Not by cutting off, but by Christ-like, gentle, gracious, wise instruction; or by reproof, as the case may need. To deal otherwise is grieving the Holy Spirit, the Comforter, and doing no little harm both to the excluding and the excluded, especially to the former.

To Chapman, a proper appreciation of the Christian life began at the cross of Christ, and contemplation of it was important to a proper walk before God. That is why he so much appreciated a weekly celebration of the Lord's Supper. His concept of the unity of the church meant that believers of all persuasions, provided they did not imbibe essential doctrinal error, comprised the true church and hence were free to cross denominational lines in seeking fellowship and worship. He believed that *life* in Christ, not the degree of understanding of Scripture—as important as that is—is the common bond in Christ.

Prophecy

In Chapman's day the subject of prophecy was popular among many Christians. Although he occasionally preached on prophecy, he seems not to have given it much prominence, in contrast to many preachers who gave the subject overriding importance. Perhaps he felt that too much ink and pulpit time were being devoted to a subject in which much interpretation was speculative and that such speculation was taking away time and energy from other essentials of the Christian life.

There are a number of reasons for suggesting this. By 1826, while Chapman was still at John Street Chapel in London, Henry Drummond—who had built John Street Chapel in 1818 for Harington Evans—had come under the influence of Edward Irving, the dynamic Presbyterian preacher. Irving's large hall in Regent Square was but a short walk from John Street Chapel. His principal interest at that time was prophecy. Having espoused a theology that denied Christ's sinless humanity, Irving was soon forced out of the Presbyterian church in disgrace. Drummond was so enamored by Irving's thinking that he decided to convene a series of conferences on prophecy at his estate in Albury, southwest of London. But during the next four years these conferences degenerated into much senseless speculation. If Evans, Chapman, or others at John Street Chapel did not attend these conferences, they certainly knew about them, and Evans publicly denounced the Irvingite teachings during this period and later.

When the Albury conferences ceased, Lady Powerscourt in Ireland decided to sponsor a similar series on prophecy. These lasted from about 1831 to 1835. Irving attended the first one or two, then dropped out when men such as Darby and Bellet—who by then had become interested in prophecy—began asserting themselves. Müller and Craik attended the 1832 conference, but Chapman apparently attended none of them. Whether the memory of the excesses at Albury was fresh in Chapman's mind is a moot point, but his absence at these conferences that attracted so many others suggests that he believed such concerns were not fundamentally important.

Although Chapman did not, apparently, take a clear position on the millennial period during his first few years of ministry, he did later on. Like most of his peers among the Brethren, Chapman made a careful distinction between the millennium of Revelation 20:4-7 and the final perfect state—the new creation. But his view of the millennium, in contrast to the view of many, was not that of universal peace. Consider these words:

> The next coming time is only a glorious porch to what lies beyond, and we ought to consider it more distinctly than we do. If Scripture were more accurately read, we should see that the golden sceptre of Christ's rule on earth will be more excellent in its nature than in its extent. Any thought of universal peace throughout the world will not bear the test of Scripture. That the nations will learn war no more will be true only of those who learn from Israel to love God. Israel's faith will be as great then as their unbelief has been in the past: they will practice no arts of war, nor will they build walls round their towns and villages. Those nations that learn of Israel will be like Israel; but my persuasion is that for those outside the limits of the golden-sceptre rule, it will be the dominion of the iron rod, according to Psalm 2, to break in pieces and consume, even till the setting up of the great white throne. The

millennial state also is a corruptible state, whereas the new creation will be incorruptible.

Chapman, together with George Müller and a small number of other leaders among the Brethren, did not believe that the Scriptures told of a secret rapture of all believers before a period of great tribulation on earth. They believed that the church as a whole must go through the period of tribulation. William Hake did not agree with Chapman's views and once told Chapman of a conversation he had with someone who was assured that the Lord might come (initiating the rapture) at any moment. Chapman replied, "Well, brother Hake, I am ready, but it's not in the Bible."

In the mid-1890s Chapman dictated his thoughts on prophecy and the rapture to E. S. Pearce, his principal fellow laborer during the last decade of his life. Many copies were printed under the title *Suggestive Questions* and distributed among his friends. Chapman's good friend Henry Dyer did not agree with him and wrote a careful, very technical response that is preserved but has not been published. In 1925 William Marriott asked Pearce for permission to publish *Suggestive Questions* and this request was granted. Pearce's reply to Marriott is interesting:

> The 14 questions were dictated to me by beloved R. C. C. when on holiday at Ilfracombe. I have also conversed with Mr. Lang [a prominent writer on Biblical themes] with respect to future events, and found he was very much in agreement with Mr. Chapman's views. That Mr. C. firmly held there would be a selection and that he—to use his own words to me—so sought to walk in obedience to the whole revealed will of God that he might not shut himself out from the honor of being one of these, and that he failed to see from other Scriptures any promise held out to the whole of the people of God being removed from the earth at the Lord's coming.

Thus Chapman believed in the partial rapture of the Lord's people.

In spite of the fact that most of his friends did not agree with his views on prophecy, Chapman saw no reason to change. He had come to a "settled judgment" on the matter, but he did not believe it was important to convert people to his interpretation of prophetic Scriptures. He realized in fact that his views were potentially divisive because the other elders at Bear Street Chapel favored the any-moment-rapture interpretation. In 1896 ninety-three-year-old Chapman called a meeting of the elders. "I have called you together," he said, "to explain that I shall not create dissension by teaching the opposite view in the Assembly." Chapman knew the difference between the essential doctrines of the Christian faith and those not essential to a saving faith. He did not permit his ego to defend nonessential, inferential doctrine at the expense of unity.

The Temptation of Christ

A common question in the nineteenth century is still asked today: Since Christ did not have a sinful nature, how could He be tempted? Another question is closely related: Could Christ have sinned? Chapman answered in this way:

> To an unregenerate person temptation cannot cause pain of a heavenly or spiritual kind; to one born of God it does. The more like God His child is, the more keenly he feels temptation to sin. To the Son of God—who was holy, harmless, undefiled, and undefilable; who was separate from sinners; who knew no sin; who was without sin—the darts of temptation must have been inexpressibly painful. He suffered, being tempted, and in that He was tempted He is able to succor them that are tempted, who, being born of God, can feel, as the unregenerate cannot feel, the pain of being tempted to evil. There was nothing in the Lord Jesus to respond to temptation.

Discipline among Believers

Regarding discipline in the church and dealing with doctrinal error, Chapman was quite willing to take firm action. One leader at Bear Street, whose speaking had been encouraged by Chapman, had moved toward the position that the punishment of the wicked was not eternal. Chapman and Hake counseled him on this, pointing out where the Scriptures speak of eternal punishment. Pride would not let the man change his position and he insisted on promoting it in the Assembly. Finally the elders at Bear Street excluded him from fellowship there. This brother eventually did see the falsity of his position, repudiated it, and was welcomed back.

We learn of Chapman's thoughts concerning those who teach false doctrine in a letter to George Müller, written jointly with William Hake in 1871:

> It is with a tender heart towards erring brethren, and a spirit of self-judgment at the mercy-seat, that we write concerning the weighty matters of false doctrine on which we lately conversed with you....We cannot but look with grief and holy indignation at the now wide-spreading doctrine which limits the duration of the punishment of the wicked. Towards the erring ones we have the bowels of Christ; with the error we would deal with iron hand....Let us use all gentleness...in showing...how great the folly...which would bind the hands of God's justice and limit the duration of the punishment of the wicked. Our intercessions must follow our admonitions. Yet if all ways of gentleness...be set at nought, then in faithfulness to the Lord and kindness to the erring ones we must, as touching fellowship, "avoid them" and "reject them," for they do the part of the heretic.

Chapman, who received no satisfaction when a difficulty in the Assembly was resolved by excluding the offending person, continued to pray for the person. Exclusion,

173

never a happy event, was a last recourse when the person refused to repent and when retaining him in fellowship constituted a positive danger to the spiritual well-being of the Assembly. On one occasion an excluded man became bitter and vowed never to speak a word to Chapman again. Sometime later they found themselves approaching each other on a street. Knowing all that the man had been saying about him, Chapman embraced him and said, "Dear brother, God loves you, Christ loves you, and I love you." This action broke the man's animosity; he repented and was soon breaking bread at Bear Street Chapel.

Obedience to Christ

Sincere Christians sometimes disagree on the role of obedience to Christ. Is it a prerequisite to salvation? Is it the litmus test of salvation? According to Chapman, "All the religion of the natural man turns the Bible upside down; it begins with works and then leads man to hope for mercy, whereas the Bible begins with the pardon of sin and then enjoins obedience." In a letter dated 1884 he wrote:

> Not one of a thousand would seem entitled to share in the rule of the heavenly kingdom, did the title hang upon walking in the Spirit....In John 17 Christ...does not distinguish between one measure of obedience and another, among the children of God; He only makes mention of the unspeakable difference between the world of [unbelievers] and those that are born from above. Yet the equity of God is seen in that each member of Christ will have his due place and office in the kingdom, that is, the place for which his obedience will have prepared and fitted him....The title to share the glory and dominion of the Lord in His kingdom...hangs upon sonship, oneness with Christ, not on the measure of obedience.

Service

When Chapman counseled young believers who were eager to serve the Lord, he urged them to prepare themselves for any service to which God might lead them, to heed the advice of older Christians, and to meditate prayerfully on the Scriptures. He discouraged haste in giving up present occupations. Writing of a young missionary, Chapman said:

> That dear youth came to me when he had begun to think solemnly of serving Christ in Africa. I counselled him to wait on God until by the Spirit of Christ he had attained to such an assurance of God's guidance as could never afterwards be by himself questioned. The cry of China for help was set before him, and brought him for a brief season trial of spirit; but soon the trial issued in full confirmation of his purpose to preach Christ in Africa.

Robert Chapman's theology had its roots in the whole Bible. He played down speculative and inferential issues and was firm on matters in which the Scriptures are clear. Some people seem to lack the ability to see things from others' perspectives. Chapman was not one of those. He was sensitive to the feelings of people who disagreed with him and upon finding himself in the minority on nonessential doctrines, he did not cause division by insisting that his views were best.

Portraits of Robert C. Chapman late in life.

20
The Best Days of His Life

During his last decade Chapman often said that those were the best days of his life. He had often prayed that his last years might be his best and God answered His servant's prayer. Chapman reminded his friends that "the present times are the best for all of us; since our lot is cast in them, there is abundant grace to enable us to fully please God." He determined not to become a crotchety old man who just looked back at opportunities lost or what might have been. There was still abundant grace for living and pleasing God, and Chapman sought to serve the Lord as long as he was physically able.

During Chapman's final years three houses were used as the Chapman rest home. Besides No. 6 and No. 9 New Buildings Street (which were probably owned then by the Grosvenor Street Chapel), No. 8 New Buildings, adjacent to Chapman's residence, had been purchased to accommodate the needs of his many guests. People often remarked that the homes were very comfortable and well furnished. By then a number of paid helpers were required to take care of the visitors, but the funds for the houses, helpers, furnishings, and food came from donations and possibly from fees or rent paid by tourists. Chapman never requested payment from the Lord's servants.

When is a man old? For Chapman it surely was not until he was in his upper nineties. He took a regular turn at preaching at Bear Street Chapel—perhaps by then it was called the Grosvenor Street Chapel—until his ninety-eighth birthday, and led or participated in three evening Bible studies each week. Scarcely a day passed without someone calling on him to seek his counsel. Requests for prayer came from all locations and Chapman was pleased to spend his time in intercession—"my chief business now"—both for friends and those unknown to him. When Henrietta Soltau was about to visit China, he wrote: "I cannot but rejoice with you in your resolve to see fellow-laborers in China. They all, with dear Brother Hudson Taylor, have been ever in my heart at the throne of grace." He interceded daily for that work until the end of his life.

As he entered his nineties, Chapman had to limit his traveling, but he kept up an active correspondence. He had become quite close to his only remaining sibling, his younger sister Arabella, who lived a few hours' journey away in Clifton. He had not lost his poet's heart, for in a letter written to her when he was ninety-two, he said, "I must sing you a song lately given me." Then he penned a poem of four stanzas and ended with this comment: "Your heart, beloved Arabella, will sing with mine."

He remained cheerful and in remarkably good health. At age ninety-three he wrote, "It is well with me—well indeed—for as I draw near the goal of my race, the Lord Jesus Christ is more and more endeared to my heart by the Holy Spirit of God." At ninety-four he wrote, "Together with constant freedom from all ailments of body, my rest in God and in Christ is such as makes things heavenly and eternal ever present, filling me with joy in God."

In an undated letter probably written during his ninety-fifth year, Chapman wrote to Arabella: "At a small outlay I have gained great wealth. I was shut up a few days in my chamber by the indiscretion of laying aside a winter garment, but while shut up—shut up with God—I saw, with keener eye of faith than heretofore, Christ my great High Priest at the right hand of God." Later in this letter he added, "I am now for a fortnight at South Molton [a town a dozen miles from Barnstaple] to give resting time from much hard work to our dear, godly servants." Even then he assisted other workers in the area.

In 1898, responding to one who had written to ask permission to name his youngest child after him, Chapman wrote: "Let prayer and reading the Word [become] so settled as to become a golden chain that no craft or power of Satan can ever loose or break. By treading this path from my youth upwards, I am now, in my ninety-sixth year, spending my days in pleasures."

In spite of his age Chapman still corresponded with missionary friends in Spain too. In January 1899 he wrote: "To my dear and loving brethren at Barcelona, Corunna, Vigo, Cartagena, Madrid, Linares, and elsewhere in Spain, who so lovingly have remembered me on my ninety-seventh birthday…. It is every way well with me…. That at my age I should be wholly free of any infirmity of the outer man carries with it great accountability." Neither had Chapman lost touch with relatives who were the offspring of his brothers and cousins. In 1899 he wrote to a kinsman, R. B. Chapman, thanking him for a gift of fruit and adding: "I am looking forward to seeing you here again this summer….I continue without any infirmity of the outer man that commonly attends old age."

J. Norman Case said that when he visited Chapman in June of 1900, Chapman told him that during the first years of his Christian life he had become convinced that God was going to spare him to an old age—for His service. Chapman thus resolved that when he was old, he would not be prevented from spiritual service because of bodily infirmity. This explains why Chapman was so diligent throughout his life to take early morning walks and baths.

During the summer of 1901 a man who only signed the initials *E.S.* and who was not a close acquaintance of Chapman, arrived for an extended stay at Chapman's home. His impressions of the ninety-eight-year-old man show that the habits of the elderly Chapman were not much different from those of his youth:

> He rises usually about 3 a.m., takes a cold bath, and spends the rest of his time till 6:30 in reading the Scriptures and intercessory prayer, then taking a morning walk in company with Mr. Pearce (his true helper) and any of his friends who were disposed to go, for about twenty minutes....After the [noon] meal he rests till 2:30 p.m. usually, being then open to receive callers, either from outside or friends staying in the house, who seek his counsel and advice on various matters. He partakes of tea at 6 p.m., and retires generally a little after 8 p.m....
> On Lord's Day, instead of appearing exhausted after his [Saturday] fast, at his advanced age, he seems fresher than ever. I heard him exclaim, with exuberant joyfulness, to one of his friends, "The Lord is risen indeed, my brother; the Lord is risen indeed!" He comes to breakfast on such occasions with his soul filled and bubbling over with heavenly matters of praise and thanksgiving, which he pours into the ears and hearts of his listeners at the table. He is most entertaining, keeping up a genial and edifying conversation with his friends, and laughing very heartily when any amusing anecdote is related to him....The beams from his cheerful countenance fall upon all alike, he having no favorites. "To have young brethren around me is one of my greatest comforts in my old age," he would often remark.

E. S. also described the Bible studies which continued in 1901:

> The subject for study on Tuesday is generally left for anyone to suggest, while Friday evening is spent in reviewing the subject taken for the [Thursday] District Meeting. In this meeting Mr. Chapman is seen in best form, his faculties being especially active, and his interest so keen and so

well maintained throughout. The meeting is opened by singing a hymn, then usually Mr. Chapman leads in prayer. Mr. Saunders then reads the portion of Scripture to be studied, following with a brief exposition of the whole. Then Mr. Chapman and he will together enlarge on the subject; following this, the meeting becomes somewhat conversational.

Saunders, then an elder at Grosvenor Street Chapel, assumed the role that William Hake had taken for many years. E. S. continued:

> After breakfast the household, including the servants, assemble in the dining room for family worship, which consists of singing a hymn, then Mr. Chapman reads a portion of Scripture and expounds it, and closes by prayer.... I well remember one day at dinner the conversation was upon our coming state in the Glory. "I shall not be in such a high position as you," one of his lady friends remarked. I shall not easily forget his pained expression; he dropped his knife and fork, his face was tinged with color, and he said, with great emphasis, "My dear sister, I feel like rebuking you; you do not understand the position at all; we are all members of His Body and one of another, and in the Glory the hand will not make any such reflection because it is not doing the work of the foot; we shall all be in our right place, and not one member out of place, and we shall be thoroughly satisfied with His arrangement."

The ninety-eight-year-old man, still mentally vigorous, had not lost his enthusiasm for languages either. E. S. recorded that during his visit Chapman was happily engaged in teaching a long-term visitor, a Swiss national, how to speak and write English correctly.

At the entrance of the twentieth century Chapman had become an almost legendary figure. His plentiful snow-white hair and beard made him look like the "patriarch of Barnstaple," as many called him. He was the only one left of the original group—Chapman, Groves, Hake, Paget, Müller, Craik, Darby, Cronin, Congleton, and many others—that had been so instrumental in starting a new and distinctive way of meeting together for worship. By this time thousands of churches throughout the world were meeting in this manner and were loosely associated through conferences, literature, and shared speakers. The aged Chapman was a connection to the historic past and many people came to Barnstaple just to see him, many out of curiosity.

Chapman delivered his last sermon at Grosvenor Street Chapel just before his ninety-eighth birthday; it lasted an hour and a quarter. On his ninety-ninth birthday in 1902 he received congratulatory messages from all over the world. A reporter for the Barnstaple newspaper ended a long article written for the occasion with these words: "Not the least of Barnstaple's claims to distinction is that she has been identified with the unique life-work of this scholar, saint, author, and preacher." Chapman spent the day simply; for a great part of it he was in his workshop making platters for his friends.

At the end of May 1902 Chapman traveled again to nearby South Molton to assist and encourage Christians there. He returned home in good health. On June 2 he rose as usual but did not feel well. A slight stroke in the afternoon rendered him physically helpless but still mentally alert. Word spread quickly. G. Hake of Bideford (William Hake's son) came to help the Pearces, as did E. H. Bennett from Cardiff. G. Fisher, who had often traveled with Chapman, and R. F. Idenden, one of Chapman's helpers during that last decade, also came to minister to him. Chapman lingered for ten more days, always comforting those who came to comfort him. People gathered in an around-the-clock vigil, recording every word he uttered. "His heart is full of the Scriptures," said one of those in attendance. On the day before he died he dictated to Mr. Pearce a statement to be read at the annual fellowship meeting at Barnstaple: "I bow to the sovereignty of God my heavenly Father; I have no will but His. We know that God is love, and if, with love of which there is no measure, there be conjoined wisdom which makes no mistakes, what becomes us, His children, but to be full of thankfulness. We have the whole heart of Christ; it is all ours."

On June 12, 1902, Robert Cleaver Chapman, God's servant, went to his rest. It had been his desire to be buried in Barnstaple, the land of his work, rather than back in Yorkshire, the land of his earthly family. Agreements had been reached long before his death that he would be buried in the same gravesite as Elizabeth Paget, his fellow worker who had died nearly forty years earlier. By law the state could have appropriated that site for a second burial twenty-one years after the first, for two burials per site were common. But no official had made an effort in that direction. So those two workers share a common grave and tombstone, which says simply, "God is Love."

The shared grave and tombstone of Robert
Chapman and Elizabeth Paget.
(photo courtesy of the author)

About two thousand people from throughout the British Isles and the continent came to his funeral. All shades of creed were represented. With so many people, it was impossible to keep the service simple. Only a few of the many capable speakers in attendance could be given the time to address the crowd, and only a fraction of the people could fit into the large meeting room at Grosvenor Street Chapel where the funeral was officially held. Several of Chapman's hymns were sung during the service. The townspeople and the many other visitors bid farewell as his body was transported from his house at New Buildings to Grosvenor Street Chapel, then from the chapel to the cemetery about a mile away. People took turns carrying the coffin—about eighty in all. Barnstaple, which had been preparing to join in joyful celebration of the coronation of King Edward, now found itself in sorrow at an open grave.

But funerals are for the living, not the dead. Chapman did not want people to dwell on his death or even his life. He wanted people to dwell on their Savior. He had purposely destroyed nearly all the letters he had received through the years from all parts of the world so that people could not say much about him. Thus, far less is known and written about Chapman than about most of his contemporaries. One of Chapman's many poems expresses his sentiments:

Beloved! why garnish the tombs of your dead?
Why grave ye the name on the stone?
Behold how the traveller rests in his bed,
His pilgrimage finished, right well has he sped,
To Jesus the spirit is gone!

The finger of Mercy has written each name
In durable letters of blood;
Go, read it by faith in the Book of the Lamb,
The record for ever and ever the same,
Laid up in the bosom of God!

J. Norman Case of China Inland Mission wrote a tribute

to Chapman in July 1902 shortly after Chapman's death. In the tribute Case said:

> In him missionaries in China and other lands have lost a real friend and constant helper at the throne of grace....It is truly marvellous how many lives were directed into and helped forward in paths of grace and godliness through the ministry and example of this one man. In Canada, in Australia, in China, as well as in many parts of the British Isles, we have met men and women who, in spite of opposition and scorn from friends, from professing Christians and the world, were pressing on in the...paths of New Testament church order, unworldly living, and self-denying service, largely nerved thereto by the consistent life of our departed friend.

Case continued:

> In June 1901...I saw our venerable brother for the last time....At the Yearly Fellowship Meeting, Mr. Chapman occupied most blessedly nearly an hour in addressing the large company of believers there gathered....During that same visit I had the privilege of going with him to see a man, ill in body and mind, who had sent for him. The man was not one of Mr. Chapman's usual hearers, but he had watched his godly, humble, self-denying life for many years. Now, in the hour of need, the only man in the town he wished to see and was willing to have speak to him about spiritual things was Mr. Chapman. The aged patriarch, then in his 99th year, leaning on my arm, walked some distance to speak words of grace and truth to the stranger who had sent for him....He also prevailed upon us to stay a day longer that he might have the opportunity of hearing of the work in China. He claimed this on the ground that he was a partner in the work, regularly remembering us in prayer for years.

An incident sometime after Chapman died nicely summarizes his character. Many people wanted to have mementos from among his possessions. His friends agreed that the fairest method would be to have his housekeeper decide how his personal possessions would be distributed. His desk, chair, clothes, and personal effects were distributed in this way. Fred Idenden told a guest about the memento he had received. It was one of Chapman's nightgowns. A few months after Idenden had acquired the nightgown, he decided to show it to someone and reminisce, but he couldn't find it. After some thought he realized that he had placed it on a pile of clothing that was sent to a mission station in Rhodesia. By now the nightgown had been given to one of the natives. Idenden pictured a happy man wearing the only memento he had received. He lamented his lost treasure, then said, "But Mr. Chapman would've liked that!"

21
Robert Chapman's Legacy

When Robert Chapman left this world to dwell in Heaven, what did he leave? Certainly not many material possessions: only his clothes, some furniture, his tools, and some kitchenware. What he left behind was far greater: an example of one who *lived* Christ.

Chapman said that the man of God is one who makes it the business of his life to please God. This definition fits Chapman well. Pleasing God and living Christ were his objectives. Striving toward those goals enabled him to become a true leader—that is to say, a servant-leader. His long life of service and concern for others testify to his Christlike character. He was indeed an apostle of love.

So many people were touched by him that fame was inevitable. But he became famous against his wishes. He could have been a prominent religious writer, but he turned down many flattering offers from publishers. He resolutely set himself against doing anything that would bring his personality into prominence. His sayings were compiled by friends without his knowledge, and he agreed to the publication of *Choice Sayings* only with the understanding that all proceeds would go to missions. He did prepare and send to press his *Hymns and Meditations,* but he did so to provide financial help to a needy local printer. We may be disappointed in his reluctance to publish and his decision to destroy his personal papers, but these decisions were simply a true reflection of his personality.

A Man of Active Faith

Although he was one of the pioneers of a religious reawakening, Chapman denied founding a new school of religious thought or recovering lost truths, as some had suggested. His insights came from long years of devoted Bible study. He began studying in earnest when he was about sixteen and continued to study the Bible, often many hours a day, during the next eighty-four years. This was the source of his spiritual strength as well as his knowledge of God's will. Prayer was his constant business. He prayed in all activities and spoke to God on all matters. Some said that when Chapman sat around a table to study the Bible with others who might well be accounted great students, he towered above them all. Henry Dyer once likened Chapman's ministry of the Word to an eagle taking flights in the heavens. He was above the clouds. "You can only catch sight of him occasionally," Dyer said. He added, "Robert Chapman in his preaching distributed nuggets of gold....These nuggets the hearers had to beat out for themselves, and the more they were beaten, the more was seen in them."

Chapman's ministry began at John Street Chapel, then expanded to Ebenezer Chapel, then to all Barnstaple, then to the surrounding areas of North Devon. Soon his missionary interests gave him influence in many countries. Because of his love and wisdom he found himself at the forefront of a movement that sought a simple form of worship and direct teaching from the Bible. By the end of his life he was known by people in all corners of the earth.

Chapman did not expect others to copy his particular lifestyle of dependence on God's provision for his material needs, but he did want Christians to live out the faith granted them and believe that dependence on God's help should not be unusual. He took to heart the promise, "The Lord will provide" (Genesis 22:14, NASB), and the Lord did provide for him and his work.

A PURVEYOR OF GOD'S WISDOM

Chapman's great love of Christ was reflected in his actions and attitudes toward people. He had a great concern for their material as well as spiritual welfare and was able to love and care for people when they were unlovable. He realized, however, that Christlike love does not mean that it is necessary to *please* everyone. He once said, "My chief desire is to please Him. If I please my brethren, I am glad. If I fail, I am not disappointed."

God used this yielded man to shepherd His flock, to teach believers and unbelievers, to heal wounds, and to restore and refresh His workers. God gave him godly wisdom and the ability to deal wisely with men. One selection from *Choice Sayings* reads, "If love see a fault, love will reprove in faithfulness the fault it sees. I say sees, for love is discerning." He defined love this way: "The love we speak of is meek and lowly; behaves itself wisely and edifies; bearing with the foolish and self-conceited, while it shuns their folly."

Thus many people and churches sought his counsel. He was so unbiased that people had great confidence in his wise counsel, which kept many families and churches together. His wisdom and intercession in prayer was part of the spiritual strength of the Müller orphanages in Bristol and the China Inland Mission of Hudson Taylor. At the time of Chapman's death there were some eighty closely-knit churches throughout North Devon—probably the greatest density of Assemblies in the world. These were known for their love and open spirit, largely due to Chapman's example and constant intercession.

189

An Apostle of Love

Chapman was not renowned as a theologian, yet he had a profound grasp of Scripture. He did not become a famous hymn writer, although he composed many excellent hymns. He was not a famous orator, although he had a magnificent voice. He did not gain acclaim as a preacher, although his peers recognized his excellence and his preaching reached the hearts of thousands.

Robert Chapman became famous for his exceptional love, grace, and truth. He became so well known in England that a letter from abroad was delivered correctly to him, addressed only to "R. C. Chapman, University of Love, England." He became famous as an apostle of love.

This servant of God was sound in doctrine and right in attitude. Love touched all his actions and this love sprang from his devotion to Christ. God has, in Robert Chapman, given us an example of a man who lived out the Christian life.

Appendix A

Robert Chapman's Family History

T he area from which the Chapmans sprang had a lonely, isolated, natural beauty. Countless generations of hardy people had lived in the villages scattered among the rocks and cliffs along the northeastern coast of England. They had built their ships in the harbors, plied their trade on the sea, and taken their food from it. Behind the coastline the land rose steeply to the west, ascending to a high plateau—the moors—treeless and silent and fog-swept, stretching back many miles. Streams that formed high in the moors joined to become the Esk river, which swept down through steep valleys and finally sliced between two high bluffs to meet the North Sea. There it created a harbor where craftsmen came to build their boats and ships. When the sun broke through the clouds over the North Sea, it shone on their whitewashed houses along the shores of the harbor, and so the people called their haven Whitby—the white village.

The Port of Whitby has secured its place in history. In

eighteenth-century Whitby, Captain James Cook was apprenticed to the sea and all four of his great ships were built there. The Scoresbys and those who accompanied them during their explorations of the Greenland seas learned their craft there. And long before their time, Caedmon—Britain's first poet—sang his famous hymn at the Whitby monastery that lay atop one of the bluffs overlooking the harbor.

It was in the Whitby area of North Yorkshire that the Chapman clan grew and prospered. Records show that Chapmans settled in the area during the reign of Henry III, before 1277. The family earned its surname from the fact that its earliest members were "chapmans"— buyers and sellers of merchandise. In those days a Robert Chapman, merchant of York, was empowered by the king of England to voyage to Denmark "to buy corn there as there is so great a scarcity in England." This charge was accompanied by a letter of commendation to the king of Denmark.

During the eighteenth century the Chapman family fairly dominated the area around Whitby. Most of the Chapmans were connected in some way to the sea. They were import-export traders, ship owners or builders, officers in the Royal Navy, sailmakers, and outfitters. Enterprising, prosperous, and prolific, the family had many branches by 1800. The Chapmans started the first bank in Whitby. Some of them became industrialists and engineers; others turned to big-game sporting in Africa. Judges, members of Parliament, and rectors of the Church of England could be found among them.

The Religious Society of Friends—the Quakers—began during the ascendancy of the Chapman family. In 1647 George Fox began preaching on what he called the "inner light of Christ." He emphasized inward spiritual experiences rather than specific creeds and preached that the Holy Spirit's guidance was more important to a person's conduct than the Bible. This type of teaching was new to most Britons and quickly attracted many of them. The Church of England did not at that time emphasize portions of Scripture that taught the working of the Holy Spirit in the individual. Clearly filling a gap in people's spiritual lives, Quakerism grew rapidly.

George Fox's influence came quickly to Whitby. In 1659 several Quaker converts purchased a piece of land at the edge of town and dedicated it as a burial ground. By 1689 William Chapman—a contemporary of George Fox—had declared his conversion to Quakerism.

The Quakers became the dominant religious force in Whitby during the eighteenth century and most of the Whitby Chapmans converted. Official Quakerism, however, forbade bearing arms for any reason, which created a difficulty for those who owned ships and needed to arm them against ships of other countries or against privateers. A historian of the Whitby Literary and Philosophical Society related, "It is said, not improbably, that the secession of the Chapmans [from the Society of Friends] was caused by their having to choose between chartering their ships to the Government—in which case the ships would have to carry guns—or remaining members of the Meeting, and they decided, apparently, in favor of the former alternative."

Thus many of the Chapmans and other Quakers were removed from official membership, but that did not stop them from considering themselves to be Quakers. Some of them established a new and less strict meeting in a village a few miles north of Whitby. Abel Chapman, William's son and R. C. Chapman's great grandfather, stayed in Whitby. Disowned by the Quakers and denied use of their burial ground, Abel built for himself and his family a handsome burial vault on a small plot that bordered the burial ground. A generation later the local Quakers had assimilated the plot, which suggests that some kind of reconciliation took place.

The relationship of the Whitby Chapmans to the Quakers and the Church of England during this time is not clear. One of Abel's sons, John, was married in a ceremony performed within the Church of England, but his children were listed in the Quaker record of births for Whitby. Thomas Chapman was one of those children and later his children (including the subject of this book) were also listed in Quaker records. The words "not in membership" or "not in unity" were attached to Thomas's name and to the names of his children. But since his children were listed in the Quaker records even though some of them were christened during Church of England ceremonies, there evidently were members of the larger Chapman family who were still Quakers and wanted the children's names maintained in Quaker records. The religious orientation of the Thomas Chapman family into which Robert Cleaver Chapman was born thus seems ambiguous.

The Chapmans operated a prosperous merchandising business in Elsinore, Denmark, during the late eighteenth century. Thomas Chapman assumed responsibility for it after he married in 1791. The living arrangements in Elsinore were comfortable and the family had many old connections in that country. So Thomas took his young wife, the former Ann Cleaver, and settled on the coast of Denmark just across the strait from Sweden.

Babies came rapidly after Thomas and Ann moved to Elsinore. The first was Ann, born in 1793. Then came John, Edward, and William, who were each born about a year apart. Next born was Thomas, who died in infancy. On January 4, 1803, Robert Chapman was born, the sixth of ten children. After him came Henry, Jane, another Thomas, and lastly Arabella, born in 1814.

THE FOREBEARS OF ROBERT CLEAVER CHAPMAN

Robert Chapman	15?? —1607
John Chapman	1570—1614
Robert Chapman	1603—1685
William Chapman	1646—1720
Abel Chapman	1694—1777
John Chapman	1732—1822
Thomas Chapman	1766—1844
Robert C. Chapman	1803—1902

Appendix B

Evans, Müller, Groves, Craik, Paget

Robert Chapman had a name for being an independent thinker, a reputation that grew with time. He would not come to a position until he was convinced of its compatibility with Scripture. Sometimes his positions on minor points were at variance with those of his good friends, but this does not mean that his friends did not influence him.

Chapman's early attitudes about Christian practice and church procedure were most heavily influenced by Harington Evans. But after arriving in Barnstaple in 1832, Chapman had extensive contact with several Christian leaders who shared many of his attitudes and helped to shape them. Robert Gribble, Thomas Pugsley, and William Hake were discussed in the text in some detail. This Appendix gives further details of the lives and ministries of Harington Evans, George Müller, Norris Groves, Henry Craik, and Elizabeth Paget and their connections to Chapman.

195

Harington Evans continued to support and encourage Robert Chapman during his years at Barnstaple and their friendship deepened. The two interacted frequently and exchanged pulpits many times. Chapman sought and appreciated Evans' counsel. There was no hint of jealousy in Evans as Chapman's reputation grew. Evans' letters show how his affection and admiration for Chapman increased, and reflect his deep concern for the work in Barnstaple.

In September 1833, a year and a half after Chapman left London, Evans visited Barnstaple while on vacation. Writing back to the congregation at John Street, Evans said, "Our dear brother Chapman desires me to send you his love, his tender love, and to say that you are on his heart daily." Vacationing again in North Devon late in the summer of 1835, Evans wrote:

> Next week I propose [visiting] the neighborhood of our dear brother Chapman, whom I have seen twice. His heart is full of love to you all for your kind testimony of Christian affection. He feels deeply thankful, and consents to your request of his taking my place [at John Street] for two Lord's Days. Many prayers have we offered up for that [Ebenezer] church, so dear to both our hearts.

When Evans and his wife returned to London at the end of that vacation, they stopped at Taplow where Mrs. Evans had grown up. They found a letter from Barnstaple waiting for them. Evans wrote to those at John Street:

> This day brings a letter...informing me of the dangerous illness of our beloved Brother Chapman. What a lesson as to the uncertainty of all things here below is here afforded us! It was but a little that I felt a need of the caution, lest I should glory in his strength, so strong did he seem as to bodily strength. And now...as a flower of grass which a breath of wind scattereth, so may he fade....Among those whom it has been my mercy to have known upon earth, I have seen few indeed like him; a child

196

so loving, a servant so ready, poor in spirit above most, and withal bold as a lion, and gentle as a nurse.

This is the only record we have of one of the few times when Chapman was ill. He recovered and the prayers of these saints surely were heard.

Two years later Evans wrote again from Barnstaple, expressing his deep regret that Chapman could not soon go to John Street to preach. The tone of the letter shows how much the people wanted to hear Chapman again and perhaps that there was a problem they felt Chapman could address:

Our dear brother Chapman is well; he sends you his much love. I placed your earnest request, that he would come to you during my absence, before him but he sees not his way at present to leave home. It is a great disappointment to me, I confess. I felt it more than I can express, but 'tis the Lord's will and not our will that is the right will; but he holds out the prospect of acceding to your request at some not very distant time....We are much refreshed by our visit, and see in the Barnstaple church that which has much strengthened and encouraged our souls.

George Müller came to London from Germany in 1829 to receive missionary training. Remarkably, only a month after his arrival someone told him about Norris Groves, who was preparing to go to Baghdad as an independent missionary. This account had a marked impact on Müller. He was particularly impressed by the fact that Groves was planning to go out on his own, not depending on a missionary society for his temporal needs, but leaning confidently on God for His leading and provision.

The discipline of the missionary society through which Müller trained soon made him restless and Groves' example bore heavily on him. He was unsure that he should stay with the missionary society. When he became ill, his friends and doctors told him to leave London for a while. Müller saw this as good advice and decided to go to the pleasant seaside area near the Exe river in southern Devonshire. Leaving London in June, he found a place to stay in the town of Teignmouth, about twenty miles from the ancient walled city of Exeter.

At Teignmouth he became acquainted with several nonconformist Christian men who greatly influenced his understanding of Biblical doctrines. One of these was Henry Craik, who preached regularly at a Baptist chapel in the nearby village of Shaldon. Seeing the freedom these men had in preaching from God's Word, Müller immediately wanted to share in their task. He wanted to preach, but no one asked this man with a heavy German accent to do so.

When fall came, Müller went back to London and the missionary society. His thoughts were constantly on the freedom of working for the Lord independently of any society. He heard that Groves had arrived safely in St. Petersburg on his way to Baghdad and this news only contributed to his agitation. A little more time passed, during which Müller convinced himself that it was unscriptural to wait upon a society of men to obtain an appointment as a missionary, and in December he dissolved his connection with the society. He left London and went back to Teignmouth, arriving on December 31.

Before he left, someone gave him the address of a remarkable nonconformist lady, Elizabeth Paget, who lived in Exeter. The unidentified brother with Exeter connections was probably the one who was keeping Müller informed about Groves. Three weeks after settling in Teignmouth, Müller traveled to Exeter to call on Miss Paget. She wasted no time and asked him to preach in the little chapel she had rented and furnished in nearby Poltimore. Müller accepted Miss Paget's offer without hesitation since his great passion at that time was to preach; it was Müller's first preaching engagement in the English language.

Unmarried, Elizabeth Paget lived with a younger sister Charlotte. Very much dedicated to the Lord, Elizabeth worked easily with the Christian men she knew, who affectionately referred to her as Bessie. Although a dissenter, she was not pleased with the dissenting chapels in the district. Seeing that many villagers in the area around Exeter were not being taught the gospel, but only a cold and lifeless form of Christianity in the Church of England or a rigid religion in some of the dissenting chapels, she took action by setting up a small chapel and seeking out godly men to preach in it.

By 1825 Groves had established a reputation locally for being a very saintly man, and Paget made a point of getting to know him. When Groves enrolled at Trinity College in Dublin to prepare for missionary service, he learned about several small groups of Christian men and women who were meeting regularly for prayer and Bible study. These people were dissatisfied with the state of things not only in the Anglican church in Ireland but also in the dissenting churches that had firm rules about membership. What Groves learned in one of these small groups about freedom of worship independent of official clergy, reinforced what Paget had been telling him. Soon he severed all relations with the Church of England. During the next few years Groves became a powerful voice among his peers for the unity of all believers on the basis of *life* in Christ rather than on the amount of Scriptural light they had.

Groves recalled that when Paget first approached him about preaching at Poltimore, he was horrified at the thought. Still loyal to the Church of England, he emphatically refused. But as his spiritual thinking matured, he changed his mind and became one of the regular preachers at that place, continuing until he left for Baghdad.

Paget arranged to have Müller stay with the William Hakes when he was in Exeter. The Hakes were then living in Groves' large old house, using it as a boarding school. Groves' sister Mary was helping Hake run the household of the school, and by the fall of that year she and Müller were married. She was a good wife for Müller, solidly supporting his idealism and enthusiasm.

No doubt it was Mary who showed Müller the pamphlet

Christian Devotedness, which Groves had published in 1825. This pamphlet advocated a lifestyle of simplicity and poverty, and trusting God to supply all needs. This was the lifestyle that Groves had adopted and maintained throughout his life. Groves had sent the pamphlet to many missionaries, including Dr. Robert Morrison, the pioneer Protestant missionary to China, who said that he was profoundly influenced by it. The pamphlet certainly affected Müller's attitude toward reliance on God as well.

Soon after arriving at Teignmouth Müller found opportunities for preaching at chapels in several of the hamlets in the area, including Thomas Pugsley's chapel at Hiscot in North Devon. Shortly after that, Müller accepted the pastorate of a small Congregationalist church in Teignmouth.

Congregationalists taught infant baptism and the young Müller was not patient about making changes in the church. One of his early actions at Teignmouth was to institute believer's baptism, which cost him half his salary because some of the members left when he made the change. He also set up a weekly observance of the Lord's Supper, adopted the principle of allowing anyone to share a word during that service, and finally renounced his salary, preferring instead to be supported entirely by freewill offerings. These changes all took place within two years, the total of Müller's tenure at the church.

Müller had become acquainted with Henry Craik during his earlier visit to the area. Craik had come from Scotland in 1826 at the age of twenty-one to tutor the two sons of Groves and to read the classics with the senior Groves while the latter prepared for missionary ordination at Trinity College. Craik was a scholar, preparing even at that time a Hebrew dictionary, and probably could have continued in a university environment as did one of his brothers. But God was preparing him for a greater career.

Not unexpectedly, Craik was greatly influenced by Groves and was the one who principally promulgated Groves' views after the latter left on his missionary journeys. When Groves abandoned his program of missionary ordination at Trinity in mid-1827 and broke all ties to the Church of England, he no longer needed Craik's services. Craik soon found another tutoring position in the area, this time with the wealthy John Synge, a friend of Groves. Synge subsidized the publication of Craik's Hebrew lexicon, his first scholarly work.

During this period Craik began accepting invitations to preach in nearby churches and developed a reputation as a good preacher. In April 1831 when his term of service to the Synge family was finished, Craik accepted the pastorate of a small Baptist group in nearby Shaldon. He also married at that time, but his wife died only a few months later.

Because of his preaching skills, Craik was invited in late 1831 to take the pastorate of a Congregationalist group at Gideon Chapel and was given the use of the empty Bethesda Chapel, both in Bristol. He accepted on the condition that George Müller be copastor with him, and the congregation agreed to this. They moved to Bristol in April of 1832, at about the same time Chapman came to Barnstaple.

Craik and Müller had come by invitation to Gideon Chapel, but had set many conditions, including the stipulation that they would not be salaried. Instead a box was placed in the back of the auditorium into which the believers could put money for the pastors. They had a practical reason for this in addition to their desire to trust the Lord for their provision. To them, a salary implied an undesirable dependence on the congregation and an implicit control from which they wanted to be free. Thus they were rejecting the Congregationalist principle of rule by the congregation. In fact they were leaning toward Baptist practice.

At the newly reconstituted Bethesda Chapel, Müller and Craik decided that they would not admit into full membership any applicants who had not been baptized as believers, although they would be allowed to take communion. This was done to avoid offending members who felt that not being so baptized was an act of grave disobedience. However it was not long before Müller and Craik became uncomfortable with their decision.

In August of 1836 Müller consulted with Chapman. In a logical approach to the problem, perhaps reflecting his training as a lawyer, Chapman responded that "either unbaptized believers come under the class of persons who walk disorderly, and in that case we ought to withdraw from them, or they do not walk disorderly. If a believer be walking disorderly, we are not merely to withdraw from him at the Lord's table, but our behavior towards him ought to be decidedly different...on all occasions." This reasoning settled Müller's and Craik's attitudes on this issue and on the whole question of reception to church fellowship. They decided "that we ought to receive all whom Christ has received, irrespective of the measure of grace or knowledge which they have attained unto." This was the principle under which Chapman was already operating at Barnstaple and which Groves had enunciated as well.

Müller frequently sought Chapman's legal as well as spiritual advice. In 1834 he had set up the Scriptural Knowledge Institution for Home and Abroad, a kind of financial clearinghouse for donations by Christians "to assist and establish new day schools, Sunday schools, and adult schools in which instruction is given upon Scriptural principles." But soon the plight of homeless children was pressed upon his mind and he wondered whether he should support them through the Institution. When he became convinced that the Lord would have him set up an orphanage, Müller consulted with Chapman and decided that funds would not be solicited for an orphanage. If the Lord wanted such a work to go forward, He would speak to the hearts of Christians to supply the funds. Thus began a faith work that resulted ultimately in a large and well-known orphanage system, and Chapman became one of its first trustees.

In late 1835 Chapman spent more than two months at Bristol during one of Craik's many spells of illness. Craik had lost his voice and was seriously thinking of resigning his position in the two churches in which he and Müller had only recently assumed leadership. Chapman stayed and helped with their work until Craik recovered and the crisis passed.

In 1842 Chapman was again in Bristol. He arrived at Müller's house on a Saturday evening for ministry the next day. When Müller opened the door to welcome him, Chapman handed him a small sum of money for the orphans. He did not know that donations had recently been very low and that Müller had not been able to buy bread for the orphans for the next day. An assistant was sitting in another room, ready to go out to buy bread in case someone came with a gift. The gift from Barnstaple supplied the amount needed. Müller recorded this as one of many instances in which God provided for his needs. Chapman was no doubt delighted to discover how God had used him.

Later that year Chapman made a short visit to Denmark and other parts of the continent. On his return he stopped at Bristol to tell Müller about his impressions of spiritual life in Europe. That life was not good, in Chapman's view. Christians in Germany were not as willing to leave the state church as the British Christians had been. The few dissenting groups had become very strict and separatist. Müller later remarked that one of these groups, "by their most exclusive separate views, only confirmed believers in remaining in the Establishment."

To the German believers he met, Chapman had explained the church procedures that he and his friends had developed during the last several years. But the typical reply was "It is Scriptural; you are right. But if we were to practice this, what would be the consequences? What would become of us and our wives and children?" In some parts of Germany at that time, groups actively promoting the gospel were subject to police raids, fines, and jail. Their fears were well founded, and few dared to break away into new forms of worship.

Chapman encouraged Müller to visit Germany to share with the Christians there his experiences at Teignmouth and Bristol, and to publish his *Narrative* in German. (It had recently been published in England with much blessing.)

Müller accomplished both objectives about a year later. His visit resulted in the establishment of many small Assemblies of Christians in Germany who met together—"without any rules," to use Müller's phrase—for worship, prayer, Bible study, and mutual support.

Chapman continued to assist in the work of Müller and Craik through the years. In 1845 Müller asked Chapman's judgment on the wisdom of greatly expanding the orphanage work. Funds for maintaining the work in the central part of Bristol had never been plentiful but were always sufficient. It was by no means clear that a greatly increased work would be supported, even though Müller had felt God's urging in this direction. Chapman encouraged him to proceed with the new plans. Müller recorded: "His visit was to me of great help in this particular, especially in stirring me up yet more to bring everything in connection with this matter before God. He also laid it on my heart to seek direction from God with reference to the plan of the building."

In the late 1830s Bessie Paget's sister Charlotte died. The Hakes were thinking of moving from Exeter to Bideford, about ten miles west of Barnstaple, to be responsible for a new boarding school for boys. Paget, then in her mid-fifties, decided to move to Barnstaple to help Chapman. Although she was wealthy, she bought the house at No. 9 New Buildings Street just across from Chapman's home in the poor Derby district.

Near the end of 1852 Groves returned from India. He was too sick to preach, but was able to make the rounds of his old friends. We find this entry in his diary: "I found dearest Bessie expecting me; she is better than I anticipated. There was a meeting at Bear Street, and I accompanied her, though tired and shaken with my journey from Ilfracombe. I slept at dear R. C.'s and they were all most affectionately kind. This morning we had a nice meeting. After breakfast we went over to Tusculum [the boarding school at Bideford run by the Hakes] and found our dear boys quite well." Bessie Paget was sixty-nine years old at this time. Norris Groves died a few months later.

When Bessie Paget died in 1863, the Hakes moved into her house. William Hake and Chapman continued an active ministry together for another twenty-five years. Henry Craik died in 1866 at the age of sixty-one, but George Müller lived on until 1898.

Many years of prayer and loving collaboration between these like-minded men and women produced some of the most remarkable faith-efforts that Christianity has known.

Notes

The following references (some with annotations) are my principal sources of written information about Robert Chapman:

1. *Robert Cleaver Chapman of Barnstaple* by W. H. Bennet (Glasgow: Pickering & Inglis, 1902). This and reference 2 are among the earliest and most reliable.
2. *Memorials of the Life and Ministry of Robert C. Chapman* by E. H. Bennett (Kilmarnock, Scotland: John Ritchie, 1902).
3. *North Devon Journal,* June 19, 1902 and June 26, 1902 (Barnstaple, U.K.). Contains an extensive obituary and several short memorials and articles; has many errors.
4. *The Good Shepherd and His Ransomed Flock* with a memorial of Chapman (printer unknown, about 1902).
5. Letter from J. Norman Case in the correspondence section of *The Witness* magazine, 1902. A memorial to Chapman.
6. *Recollections of a Visit to Barnstaple* by E. S. Author not further identified. (Glasgow: Pickering & Inglis, 1903?) A useful early memorial.
7. *Brother Indeed* by Frank Holmes (London: Victory Press, 1956; reprint, Kilmarnock, Scotland: John Ritchie, 1988). This readable volume contains much material not found elsewhere.
8. *England, Home and Beauty* by H. B. Macartney. Quoted in *Brother Indeed* (reference 7).
9. *A History of the Plymouth Brethren* by William B. Neatby (London: Hodder & Stoughton, 1901). Rich in information

207

about the Brethren split of 1845–1849. This and the following two references are the best books describing the Brethren movement.

10. *The Origins of the Brethren* by Harold H. Rowdon (London: Pickering & Inglis, 1967). Definitive; carefully researched and written by a professional historian.

11. *A History of the Brethren Movement* by F. Roy Coad (Exeter, U.K.: Paternoster, 1968). Carefully researched account of the Brethren principally of the nineteenth century.

12. *Chief Men Among the Brethren,* compiled by H. Pickering (first U.S. printing, Neptune, NJ: Loizeaux, 1986). Short biographies of selected Brethren, with significant omissions.

13. *The Pilgrim Church* by E. H. Broadbent (London: Pickering & Inglis, 1931). A fascinating account of the many "Brethren" movements since A.D. 300.

14. *Choice Sayings* by R. C. Chapman (Barnstaple, U.K.: John Inch Krill; revision, London: Morgan; reprint, Glasgow: Gospel Tract Publications, 1988).

15. *Hymns and Meditations* by R. C. Chapman (Barnstaple, U.K.: John Inch Krill, 1871). The hymns are also published under various titles, such as *Hymns for the Use of the Church of Christ.*

16. *Letters of the Late Robert Cleaver Chapman,* edited by J. Henry Hake (London: Echoes of Service, 1903). Includes three letters to Eliza Gilbert, the oldest of his preserved letters. Chapman's 1834 trip to Spain is known only from a footnote in this collection.

17. "Select Sayings from Several Addresses" by R. C. Chapman. An article in *The Witness* magazine.

18. *How Shall We Order the Child?* A compilation of several essays written by William Hake and edited by R. C. Chapman.

19. *Seventy Years of Pilgrimage, Being a Memorial of William Hake,* edited by R. C. Chapman (Glasgow: The Witness Office and Christian Literature Depot, 1891?).

20. *A Narrative of Some of the Lord's Dealings with George Müller* by George Müller. Privately printed in several volumes over a period of forty years beginning in the 1840s. (First part, 8th edition, London: J. Nisbet, 1881.)

21. *Passages from the Diary and Letters of Henry Craik of Bristol* by W. Elfe Tayler (London: J. F. Shaw, 1866).

22. *The Chapman Story, 1327—1954* by H. B. Browne (Whitby, U.K.: Horne, 1954). An account of the long history of the Chapman family. Much of appendix A is drawn from material found in this and the following two references.
23. "Chapman Pedigree," compiled by Joseph Foster, 1874. Original at the Whitby Literary and Philosophical Society, Whitby, North Yorkshire, U. K. Contains a nearly complete genealogy of Chapman's forebears.
24. *The Streets of Whitby and Their Associations* by H. P. Kendall (Whitby, U.K.: Whitby Literary and Philosophical Society, 1976). Contains useful information about the history of Whitby.
25. *Memoir and Remains of the Rev. James Harington Evans,* written and edited by his son, the Reverend James Joyce Evans (London: James Nisbet, 1852). Most of the knowledge of Harington Evans comes from this book.
26. *Recollections of an Evangelist* by Robert Gribble (London: William Yapp, 1857). A very brief autobiography. Suggests that the house churches and village chapels near Barnstaple were Congregational, but see the following two references.
27. "Origins of the Brethren Movement, with Particular Reference to North Devon," an unpublished dissertation by Hilary Pierce, 1974. Contains little-known information about the small churches near Barnstaple in which Gribble, Pugsley, and Chapman were influential. Suggests that some were Baptist, even Particular Baptist.
28. *A History of the Methodist Revival of the Last Century in its Relation to North Devon* by J. G. Hayman (London: Wesleyan Methodist Book Room, 1898). States that the chapel near Tawstock under Pugsley's guidance was Wesleyan (Methodist).
29. *Barnstaple Yesterday* by J. & J. Baxter (Bristol, U.K.: H. J. Chard, 1980).
30. The Fry Collection, compiled by H. H. Rowdon (reference 10). A source of Brethren documents not available until the 1960s, it is maintained in the Christian Brethren Archives at the John Rylands University Library of Manchester, Oxford Road, Manchester M139PP, U.K.
31. Letter from Amy Jane Toulmin, a cousin of B. W. Newton, to another cousin commenting on the Chapman rest home and

H. W. Soltau. Dated December 9, 1847. Surprisingly, letter mentions a cost for staying at the home. Copy at the John Rylands University Library of Manchester, Oxford Road, Manchester M139PP, U.K.

32. *George Müller and R. C. Chapman: Did They Change Their Mind as to the Coming of the Lord being After the Tribulation?* by G. H. Lang, privately printed about 1956. Copy at the John Rylands University Library of Manchester, Oxford Road, Manchester M139PP, U. K.

33. Letter from K. P. Townsend to G. H. Lang, dated September 3, 1954. Copy at the John Rylands University Library of Manchester, Oxford Road, Manchester M139PP, U. K.

34. *Suggestive Questions* by R. C. Chapman, edited by William Marriot (Norwich, U.K.: 1926?). Copy at the John Rylands University Library of Manchester, Oxford Road, Manchester M139PP, U.K.

35. "Answers by H. Dyer to Questions by R. C. Chapman," unpublished letter written about 1900. Copy at the John Rylands University Library of Manchester, Oxford Road, Manchester M139PP, U.K.

36. *A Woman Who Laughed: Henrietta Soltau, Who Laughed at Impossibilities and Cried "It Shall be Done"* by M. Cable and F. French (London: China Inland Mission). The "Homer under my pillow" remark of Chapman is found in this book.

37. *Hudson Taylor and China's Open Century* by A. J. Broomhall (London: Hodder & Stoughton, 1985). The definitive study of Hudson Taylor.

38. Notes written about 1960 by an elderly lady who as a young girl was a helper in Chapman's homes. Notes in the possession of Charles Fraser-Smith, Barnstaple, U.K.

39. 1851 ecclesiastical census of England. Copies in the Barnstaple library. The census establishes 1842 as the date of completion of Bear Street Chapel. A map of Barnstaple printed in 1843 also shows a chapel on the site at Grosvenor Street.

Sun 4/10/11
2:30 am EDT
pg.192 Henry III
c.1277
George Fox began preach.
in 1647.